My Favorite
SENIOR
MOMENTS

KAREN O'CONNOR

HARVEST HOUSE PUBLISHERS
EUGENE, OREGON

Cover design by Dugan Design Group, Bloomington, Minnesota

Cover photos © Dugan Design Group; guru3d / Fotolia

Published in association with Books & Such Management, 52 Mission Circle, Suite 122, PMB 170, Santa Rosa, CA 95409-5370, www.booksandsuch.com

MY FAVORITE SENIOR MOMENTS
Copyright © 2015 by Karen O'Connor
Published by Harvest House Publishers
Eugene, Oregon 97402
www.harvesthousepublishers.com

ISBN 978-0-7369-5960-5 (pbk.)
ISBN 978-0-7369-5961-2 (eBook)

Library of Congress Cataloging-in-Publication Data
O'Connor, Karen, 1938-
   My favorite senior moments / Karen O'Connor.
      pages cm
   1. Older Christians—Religious life. 2. Aging—Religious aspects—Christianity. I. Title.
BV4580.O375 2015
248.8'5—dc23

                                                                    2014021859

Printed in the United States of America

18 19 20 21 22 / VP-JH / 10 9 8 7 6 5 4

To my hiking pals.

Acknowledgments

My thanks to these men and women who contributed suggestions, ideas, and their own experiences as "story seeds" that I used, with their permission, to write this book.

Phyllis Allen • Pat Baer • Diane Barker • Mary Battmer • Kris Flynn • Bill Giovannetti • Lisa Hamil • Judi Hill • Ginger Ramin Hixson • Cathy Hopper • Jade Kinnaman • Charlie Levine • Carol Nicolet Loewen • Margaret Mayhew • June O'Connor • Mary Panhorst • Donna Poole • Linda Evans Shepherd • Peggy Smith • Janet Thompson • Sherry VanZante • Sandra Victor • Peggy Sue Wells • Bess Whitaker • Dawn Wilson • Connie Bertelsen Young

*Our mouths were filled with laughter,
our tongues with songs of joy.*

PSALM 126:2

A Note from Karen

Do you, like me, sometimes look in the mirror and wonder whose face that is? You no longer see the handsome dude of 50 years ago or the glamorous gal with long red hair who was voted homecoming queen in high school. *Ack!* The years have gone by quickly, and suddenly we're facing the second half of life…or maybe the last quarter. It can be a discouraging prospect if we let it be. But it can also be one of the best seasons of our lives if we choose to make it so.

One thing always cheers me up—knowing I'm not alone. Other people are looking in the mirror too and deciding how they will live these final chapters of their lives. Will we choose love and laughter or fear and worry? I choose love and laughter! In that vein, I've compiled some of my favorite senior moments from my life and from the lives of others to help you choose the funny side of the street too.

I hope these stories and prayers encourage you to look at life from the positive, sunny side of the street so you can continue to live wholeheartedly—especially knowing that God is with you…and always will be.

Karen O'Connor
Watsonville, California

Looking Good

1

Whose Face Is That?

Louann's granddaughter Chloe was quick to tell her grand-mother she had the figure of a teenager—but then she added these dreaded words: "Well, I mean, except for your face."

That did it. Louann ran to the bathroom as soon as Chloe left for home. The sweet girl didn't mean to hurt her feelings. She was just speaking the truth. But still, it did hurt to hear it put so bluntly. Louann knew she looked older—but really old? "I'm not ready for that," she murmured to her reflection. "Lord, whose face is that in the mirror? It can't be mine. Why, it seems just yesterday that I looked like her." Louann pointed to a photo on the wall of her sister Amy and herself taken when they were in high school.

Louann moved to the living room and surveyed her wedding photo and then one of her first child, Robert, and her on his fifth birthday.

"I was a pretty good-looking chick in those days. What happened?"

"A lot," God seemed to whisper in her ear.

Louann thought about it.

- college
- marriage
- childbirth
- school
- graduation

- work
- illness
- parents' deaths
- grandchildren
- more…so much more

Life happened, that's what. And with every year, Louann had experienced a little more wear and tear. She went back to the bathroom and peered into the mirror again. She smiled this time. "It's okay. You're still young at heart, Louann. And you're still beautiful in God's eyes. And, most important, you're deeply loved!"

Today's Thoughts
See what great love the Father has lavished on us,
that we should be called children of God.
And that is what we are.

1 John 3:1

Thank you, Lord, that I'm alive at this "advanced" age. It's a privilege not everyone gets to enjoy.

2

Trashed Hopes

Manny liked to be his wife's hero. Whenever he could impress her with his prowess, he did, whether it was climbing a ladder to take down a hornet's nest, hanging a picture above the mantel, or changing the oil in her car. He also made a point of being the one to put the trash bin at the curb every Thursday night for pick up on Friday morning.

Elsie could take out the trash since the container had wheels and handles, but Manny considered this smelly, messy work—a man's job. And he did it valiantly until…

One Thursday evening he set out the can as usual and then went to bed. The next morning at six o'clock he heard the rattle and roar of the sanitation truck driving up and down the neighborhood streets, picking up the trash cans with its strong metal arms, and heaving the garbage into the large opening at the top. He knew it would take a while to get to all the homes, so he decided to turn over and catch an extra 40 winks.

At seven, Manny's eyes popped open. He glanced at the alarm clock on his nightstand. He'd overslept! He bounded out of bed—well, not exactly bounded. But he did get up and pull on his sweats, ready to retrieve the trash bin and wheel it back to the garage. This had been his routine for some 15 years. He headed outside.

When he got to the curb he stopped and rubbed the sleep from his eyes. No trash can in sight. Nada! Nowhere! *How odd*, he thought. His neighbors' containers were in place. Not one missing except his.

Manny instantly got mad. Someone had stolen his trash can! Well, whoever it was wouldn't get away with it. He'd have the individual's hide and more. And he'd report it to the cops too. What kind of neighborhood was this anyway? Why, a man couldn't even trust his neighbors! Then Manny felt guilty. His shoulders slumped as he looked at the houses on his quiet street. Good, decent people lived inside each one. And they all had their own trash cans, so why steal his?

A stranger. That's it, he decided. Someone outside the area. That had to be the case. Manny marched inside. He was a man with a mission. He had a lady inside who needed him to protect her from the thieves in the area.

When he got to the kitchen he explained the situation to Elsie, who was sipping a cup of coffee at the table. "And don't you worry, honey," Manny assured her. "I'll get to the bottom of this. There is nothing to be afraid of. I'll take care of it." His chest puffed out a bit as he reached for the phone.

Elsie leaned over and touched his arm. "Who are you calling?"

"The city offices—the Sanitation Department, that's who."

Elsie put down her cup. "I already took care of it, dear."

Manny scratched the bald spot on his head. "How'd you do that? And when?"

"This morning. I couldn't sleep with the sun streaming through the window, so I got up early and made coffee. I heard the garbage truck coming and going, so I sat and watched. I've always been fascinated with those big rigs and how they heft such heavy bins, dump them, and bring them back down to the street—all in a matter of seconds."

She smiled. "But the strangest thing happened this morning. The truck came up, grabbed our bin and lifted it up. And our bin disappeared! Then the truck drove away. I couldn't get outside fast enough to flag the driver to stop. So I called the Sanitation Department, and the customer-service person said not to worry. 'This happens sometimes,' he told me. He said he'll have a new bin sent out on Monday."

Elsie picked up her cup and sipped more coffee.

Manny put down the phone and scratched his head again. Looks like he'd have to postpone being a hero. Elsie was clearly able to take care of business.

Today's Thoughts

Cast your cares on the Lord and he will sustain you.
PSALM 55:22

Lord, I'm often preoccupied with being a hero instead of realizing that you are the only hero anyone needs. Thank you.

3

Romeo, Romeo…

Chuck had a pleasant conversation with his new friend Barney, who'd recently turned 90.

"It would be wonderful to see more of you," Barney said.

Chuck agreed. "We ought to get together for coffee some weekday since we're both retired. How about meeting downtown at Starbucks on Friday morning?"

The men picked a time and said goodbye.

Chuck was aware of how quickly time was passing. It was important to stay in touch with people he cared about—and Barney was one of them. "We never know how much time we have left to socialize with good friends," he told his wife over dinner that evening.

Later that week, the two men met for coffee and chatted about old times, solved the world's problems, and told a few corny jokes. When they were ready to part, Barney shared an idea. "Chuck, how about being my guest at a new men's club in town? You can see if you like it. If you do, you can become a member too."

"I might be interested. What club is it?" asked Chuck.

"It's called Romeo. You'll love it. After speaking with you a few days ago, I knew you'd be an ideal recruit."

Chuck felt his stomach clench. Just the name of the group chilled him. He was long past the age of even imagining himself as a Romeo. "I'm sorry, Barney," he said with a catch in his voice. He didn't want to offend his friend, but for sure he wasn't about to risk his reputation by joining such an organization. In fact, he was pretty disappointed to learn that Barney was *that* kind of man. "That doesn't sound like my kind of club." He added, "I'll stick to Toastmasters."

At Chuck's look, Barney broke out laughing—so loud, in fact, that Chuck was taken aback. Barney said, "I apologize, Chuck. You've got the wrong idea. Romeo is an *acronym*."

Chuck wasn't sure he wanted to know what the letters stood for. *Maybe ignorance really is bliss*, he thought.

But Barney didn't wait for Chuck's go-ahead. He belted out the letters and what they stood for. "R–O–M–E–O: Really Old Men Eating Out."

Then it was Chuck's turn to laugh out loud. "Count me in!" he said. "I'm all about being that kind of Romeo."

Today's Thoughts
If any of you lacks wisdom, you should ask God,
who gives generously to all.
JAMES 1:5

Lord, I'm so glad I can have fun with family and friends at this stage of life. A good belly laugh helps ease the tension and keeps me from becoming a sourpuss.

4

Happy Golden Years

Millie glanced at her reflection in the front window of Bartlett's Department Store. My, she was a sight. She needed new glasses, a new hairdo, new makeup, and a new outfit, to say nothing of a new pair of shoes—especially this week. She and Joe were going on being married 50 years now. They planned to celebrate their golden anniversary on Saturday. Millie wanted to look beautiful for her husband. They were going to restate their vows in front of their family and a few close friends. She hoped Joe would tell her she looked as beautiful as the day he married her.

Just the thought brought a flush to her cheeks. Here they were in the happy golden years of life that people always talked about. *They are golden,* Millie thought. She and Joe had a rich life filled with faith, family, friends, and plenty of opportunities for fun. They'd had their mishaps, misunderstandings, health issues, and money challenges like most couples, but they'd gotten through them. Life was indeed good.

Millie walked into the store and headed toward the escalator. She wanted to concentrate on creating a new image, but she couldn't stop thinking about the past and how quickly time was moving. Where had the years gone? She and Joe had been high school sweethearts once upon a time. Now they were 70-something seniors. They'd been together for so long they could hardly remember when they were apart.

They were as compatible with one another as a sock and a shoe.

Joe provided the sturdy exterior that shielded them from harm, and Millie lined their marriage with her love and warmth. God kept them together by his grace. They had a good life, and Millie hoped many more years were ahead.

She looked up and realized she was on the second floor—women's wear. Perfect! She wandered through the dresses and casual wear, but nothing seemed quite right. Then on the back wall she spotted a simple silk blouse with gold flecks. On the rack below was a matching skirt. She tried them on, and they seemed made just for her.

Next Millie sailed into the shoe department and purchased a pair of gold-colored sandals with little straps across the insteps. She was set. She already had gold earrings and a bracelet. Now she needed some pretty makeup, a haircut, and a perm.

Millie's heart pounded. She'd never spent money on herself like this. But it seemed right to give herself something new and pretty for such a memorable occasion. *Won't Joe be surprised when he sees me waltz into the banquet room all golden and happy,* she mused. *I'll be ready to celebrate our happy golden years on our golden anniversary!*

Today's Thoughts
Marriage should be honored by all.
HEBREWS: 13:4

Dear God, the golden years are for people who trust in you and then live life to the fullest till you call them home. May I be among them.

5

Loafin' Around

Les walked into the shoe store and scanned the shelves before settling into a chair. A young salesman strode up. Les noticed his name tag—JASON—and the braces on his teeth. The lad was wearing a smart-looking pair of jeans and blue tennis shoes.

"May I help you, sir?" the young man asked as he smiled and stuck out his hand.

"I hope so," Les said as he returned the handshake. He let out a deep sigh. "I'm getting old, son. I need some shoes I can slip in and out of without having to bend over. Trouble is, when I do bend over I have a hard time getting back up. Know what I mean?" Les looked at the salesman. "No, I guess you wouldn't know what I mean. You're too young. I bet you run track or play basketball."

"No, sir. I play chess."

"And sell shoes, I see." Les chuckled. "Getting old is a pain in the behind. You have a long way to go before you get to where I am."

The young man pulled a pair of sneakers off a shelf. "How about some canvas shoes with Velcro? No laces to tie, sir."

"But I'd still have to bend over to fasten the Velcro. I don't want to bend over." Les was aware his voice was escalating. He calmed himself down.

"Oh, that's right. Okay, let me see…" The salesman glanced at the shoe display along the wall.

"What I'd really like is a good pair of comfortable penny loafers—the slip-on kind, you know?"

"Penny loafers?" Jason said. "I'm not sure we have that. I've never heard of them, actually."

"You've never heard of a penny loafer? Where have you been?"

The young man's face turned as red as the leather chair Les was sitting on. "No worries, sir. I'll ask my manager. He's an older…I mean, he's pretty experienced in men's shoes. If we don't have them here, I'll do a search on Google for you. One of our affiliates might be able to help."

"Google? What's that?" Les asked.

"You haven't heard of Google, sir? It's a search engine on the Internet."

"A search engine on what? No, don't explain. I haven't heard of it, but I know what the Internet is. No worries though. I'll ask my grandson to explain it the next time he comes over."

Today's Thoughts
Stand up in the presence of the aged,
show respect for the elderly and revere your God.
LEVITICUS 19:32

Lord, you didn't have to deal with loafers and tennis shoes when you were on earth. A basic sandal was good enough for all occasions.

6

A Loooong Time!

Marge and Bill had been dating for some time—well, a *loooong* time. Thirteen years, actually. Marge is 93 years old and still works in the same real estate office she's been with for the past 52 years. That's a loooong time too. And Bill, at age 100, has been retired for a loooong time.

Several years ago the two signed up for a Panama Canal cruise. They're not married, so they did the proper thing. Each shared a cabin with another single person of the same gender. Every morning Marge and Bill met in the dining room for breakfast and then spent the day together. Their time together ended late into the evening—sometimes past midnight after dancing a loooong time to the music of a live band.

One night as Bill walked Marge back to her cabin, he grabbed her hand and stole a little kiss on her cheek. The two chuckled and snuggled close as they approached Marge's cabin door. Just then a woman walked by. She paused. "You two are so cute together. It's really nice to see older people show a bit of romance. It gives me hope for my husband and me. By the way, how long have you two been married?"

Bill answered without hesitation. "A loooong time—but not to each other."

"Oh, dear!" The woman exclaimed and then rushed off.

Bill and Marge cracked up.

Bill slapped his leg. "She didn't give me time to explain. She must think we're having an…"

"We are!" interrupted Marge. "An affair of the heart. And I'm certain our late spouses would be happy for us."

Today's Thoughts
Through wisdom your days will be many,
and years will be added to your life.
PROVERBS 9:11

Lord, although the time I most look forward to is being in heaven with you when my days on earth are finished, I'm glad I'm alive today.

7

The New Dress

One Thursday Evelyn bought a new dress—a sleek little number in black with a low, round neckline and a snug-fitting skirt. She had the figure to wear such a piece even at age 65. Ev and Ron had been invited to a country club dance the following Saturday night, and Ev wanted to look her best. She also made a trip to the salon for a cut, perm, manicure, and pedicure. It wasn't often these days that the two of them had an opportunity to attend a gala.

In fact, when she thought about it, life was getting a bit dull. Dinner at home most nights, followed by a couple of hours of news on CNN and maybe a sitcom or two before going to bed at 10. *What happened to romance?* Evelyn wondered as she reminisced about the good old days. The days and nights when Ron would slip an arm around her shoulder and whisper sweet nothings in her ear—the kind one heard in songs on the radio or saw in movies while holding hands and sharing a box of popcorn. She missed those times and wondered why they had to end just because they were getting older. *What can I do about this?* Ev pondered some ideas she'd read about that might light the romance fire in her husband again. She wasn't expecting frenzied and passionate love. After all, they weren't exactly kids anymore. But a bit of playful coziness would be nice once in a while.

So Ev plotted. She decided to create an evening to remember—a candlelight dinner with iced tea in wine goblets, chocolate-covered strawberries for dessert, and a romantic movie—something cute and tender about people their age—perhaps *Hope Springs* or *On Golden Pond*. She woke up on Saturday morning eager to dress up for the dinner and dance at the country club that evening. She was also excited about putting her plan in place for the romantic evening with Bill the following week.

At five-thirty Evelyn donned the last of her accessories—dangling black earrings with a touch of silver to match her silver-strapped sandals. She walked down the hallway to the living room where Ron was waiting. He looked handsome in his dark suit and red-striped tie.

"What do you think of my new dress?" Evelyn asked as she entered the room.

"New wife, you mean. You look hot!"

Hot? Ron hadn't used such a word in reference to her ever. *Hanging out with the teen grandkids, I gather,* Evelyn decided. She smiled, holding back a chuckle. *I got his attention, at least.* She pushed a bit further. "The dress? What do you think? It was kind of expensive, but I thought…"

"Here's what I think. Let's stay home!" With that comment, Ron plastered a kiss on his beautiful wife.

Evelyn reported that they went to the club as planned, and, afterward, in the privacy of their home they continued their gala evening.

Today's Thoughts
I will bless her with abundant provisions.
Psalm 132:15

Lord, thank you for taking care of all my needs, even those I'm not aware of. I praise your holy name.

8

Pretty in Purple

Rosalind invited her family to meet her for lunch at her favorite coffee shop. It would be her treat because they were going to celebrate her granddaughter Hannah's fifth birthday. Everyone, dressed up and smiling, arrived on time and settled into a large corner booth.

Rosalind's daughter Amanda took one look at her mother and nodded with approval. "Mom, you look beautiful. Purple is definitely your color. You should wear it more often."

Amanda's young son, Donny, poked his two-cents worth into the conversation. "Yeah, Grandma. Purple is a good color for you. It matches your hands."

Rosalind looked at the spider veins on her hands and laughed. "Good observation, Donny. And my dress matches my legs too."

"You mean those purple lines on your legs?"

"Umm, yes, those are the ones."

"Well, at least they go with your dress. But if you wear some other color, I think you should stick to pants, don't you?"

"Good idea!"

Today's Thoughts

Those who exalt themselves will be humbled,
and those who humble themselves will be exalted.

MATTHEW 23:12

Lord, it takes courage to hear someone—especially a child—speak so bluntly. But truth is truth. Help me humbly receive what people say and not take offense where none was meant.

9

Catch of the Day

Rose and Juliette were tired of being each other's primary companion. They enjoyed their 50-year friendship, but they longed for some manly input in their lives. They each wanted to find a man who would take them out to the movies, or to dinner, or to a concert, or for a walk in the park. Someone who would care for them, although they weren't necessarily looking for marriage—not at their respective ages of 72 and 73.

"Been there, done that," Rose said. She'd become a widow at age 31.

Juliette, on the other hand, would have welcomed a spouse. But after being single for so many years the thought of living with someone of the opposite gender frightened her. She was set in her ways. She didn't want a man—or anyone, for that matter—coming into her home and messing with her routine. A male *companion* to go out with would be just right. They'd enjoy an evening together and then say goodnight and go home to their own houses.

One Tuesday afternoon the two women met to discuss strategy for attracting the kind of men they were interested in. They considered several dating websites, including ChristianMingles, eHarmony, and Match, but they decided against dating services. They'd rather meet someone at church, the gym, through a book club, or while line dancing.

They talked over what they planned to do and then parted company, agreeing to meet the following Tuesday to compare notes.

The next week Juliette strode into the café where she was to meet Rose. Her friend looked dejected. "What a sour look," Juliette remarked. "What's wrong?"

"What's wrong is nothing. Absolutely nothing has worked for me. I've dressed up, stepped out, and started conversations, but not one man has picked up my signals or shown interest. How about you?"

Juliette beamed. "I met a man I'm interested in!"

"Where?" Rose asked.

"At Colonial Funeral Home."

"An undertaker?" Rose wrinkled her nose. "Not terribly romantic."

Juliette laughed. "Not the undertaker, silly. One of the pallbearers at my neighbor's funeral service."

Rose chuckled. "Well, you beat all. Clearly I've been hanging out at the wrong places."

Today's Thoughts

Delight yourself in the LORD; and
He will give you the desires of your heart.
PSALM 37:4 NASB

Thank you, Lord, that what I need and want comes to me when I trust you, ask you for guidance, and wait for your plan to unfold.

10

Check, Check, Check!

Barbara got out of bed, splashed some water on her face in the bathroom, and then took a brave step. She looked in the mirror. She'd been using a new anti-wrinkle cream for several weeks, and today was the day to check for results. She stretched her cheeks and prodded her eyelids. *I don't look any different*, she thought. "Another 50 bucks down the drain!" she said to her reflection in the mirror. She picked up the jar of goo and tossed it into the trash. "Take that, you hypocrite!"

Barbara was fed up with the obvious signs of aging. How crummy! She didn't feel like 71, but her face told a different story. And it didn't help her ego one bit when another volunteer at the rescue mission suggested she try the anti-wrinkle cream. Who was she to dish out advice? She was 72 and losing her hair!

Barbara sat down in the kitchen and nibbled on a banana while the coffee perked. She reached for her iPad and clicked on the Bible app. "Lord, what do you think? Am I as dreadful looking as I feel or as old as my friends indicate with their little jabs and unwanted ideas?" She did a quick search. It didn't take long to discover what mattered to God—the fact that she loved him and that he was renewing her mind and life day by day.

Today's Thoughts

We do not lose heart.
Though outwardly we are wasting away,
yet inwardly we are being renewed day by day.

2 CORINTHIANS 4:16

Dear Lord, some of these situations I encounter are down-right funny and some are down-right pathetic. I don't know whether to laugh or cry. So I'll turn to you in my disappointment, knowing you will never forget me or overlook me no matter what I do or how I look.

11

Facin' Facts

Harold walked into the hair salon aware that he needed a good cut. The small amount of hair he still had needed trimming now and then, much as he hated to part with even one strand. And he certainly wasn't going to let it grow to the point where he could wear a "comb over." No way! What were guys who resorted to such a last resort thinking? Didn't they ever look in a mirror? They probably weren't using their heads! *Hey, pretty funny!* Harold smiled at his own joke and then proceeded to the chair by the front window. This was Maggie's station. Harold knew she'd be gentle with his ego.

She said hi and draped a long cape around his neck to cover his shirt and jeans. Next she looked at his unruly clumps and ran a comb through them. "What'll it be?" she asked.

"I need a trim." Harold held Maggie's gaze. *Was she going to make a wisecrack? She wouldn't...or would she?* Harold had become so sensitive about his thinning hair that he was sure everyone who looked at him was ready to stab him with a cutting comment.

Maggie picked up her scissors and began clip, clip, clipping. Then she cleaned up his neck with an electric razor.

Harold broke the silence with a joke of his own. "How about we paste the scraps here?" He pointed to the bald spot on the top of his head.

"Nice you can joke about your condition," said Maggie. "Most men are so sensitive. I just keep my mouth shut when I'm working on a baldy."

A baldy? Is that what she thinks of me? Harold felt his face flush and his temper flare. *Easy for her to say. She's only 30 years old and has enough hair to last a lifetime.*

"No, I've learned my lesson," Maggie continued. "One guy got up and walked out on me when I made a simple comment. I didn't mean any harm at all. Just facin' facts, you know."

Harold was hooked. Now he had to hear what she'd said that had driven the man out of the shop. "What could be so terrible?" he asked.

"While I was cutting I tapped his bald spot and said, 'Hair today—gone tomorrow!'"

Harold smiled. "Yep, that would do it, all right," he quipped.

Today's Thoughts
*People look at the outward appearance,
but the LORD looks at the heart.*
1 Samuel 16:7

Lord, sometimes I am so vain—whether it has to do with my hair, or my talent, or my physical body. I'm happy to be reminded that though I must keep myself clean and in good order, you are more concerned with the condition of my heart.

12

Not Again...

Laura and her friend Cheryl decided to run a few errands together. "I need a new phone," Laura said. "Ours has gone out so it's time for a new one. Please help me remember. I'm having a lot of senior moments lately."

Cheryl agreed. She wanted to make a few stops of her own. The women joked about their forgetfulness. As Cheryl pulled into the shopping center and parked, Laura mused, "I wonder if just reading and hearing about senior moments in others makes it contagious."

Sure enough, as the women made their final stop at the electronics store, Laura started feeling jittery. She was supposed to get something here. What was it she needed? She ran through a list in her mind but nothing clicked. Cheryl walked behind her and asked, "What brand of phone do you like?"

Whew! Laura blew out a huge breath. Her friend had saved her the embarrassment of having to admit that she'd forgotten what they came for! She'd narrowly avoided having to chalk up another senior moment. She smiled as she shared her relief with her friend.

As the duo walked out to the parking lot, Cheryl broke out laughing. "Now it's my turn to forget. I hope I got what I came to the mall for!"

"Looks like we might have to go home and start all over," Laura joked. "You're sure to think of what you forgot the moment we walk in the door."

Today's Thoughts

The LORD God is a sun and shield;
the LORD bestows favor and honor;
no good thing does he withhold from
those whose walk is blameless.

PSALM 84:11

Thank you, Lord, for good friends who understand me. I also thank you for allowing me to be totally human, even with all my failings and foibles. I love knowing you take care of me no matter what.

13

A Real Donation

Marni picked up the mail and shuffled through it, separating the junk from the real thing. She let out an exhausted sigh. "So much waste," she muttered as she turned on the shredder. Just then she noticed a postcard from a local charity. A driver would be in her neighborhood in a few days, and if she put a marked bag of her discards at the curb, he would pick them up.

What a great service! Marni hated lugging unwanted items to the drop-off spot in town. Now she'd be spared that chore. The next morning she went through her clothes closet, the garage, and the kitchen, gathering up all the shoes, jackets, blouses, knickknacks, and kitchenware she no longer wanted or used. What a relief to declutter her house and, at the same time, help people in need. By the afternoon she had one large box ready to set at the curb and two large black bags, each one properly marked for the charity. When the truck arrived a few days later, Marni watched through the front window as the driver loaded her box and bags onto the truck. That was that. She felt good.

Later in the week, Marni dressed for a luncheon she and a friend had agreed to attend. She chose her lavender skirt and matching sweater. She reached into her closet for her black pumps—the new ones she'd purchased on sale at the department store just weeks before. But they weren't there. They weren't at the door where she often left her shoes when she came in from outside. Maybe they were still in the store box...no, she remembered tossing the shoebox into the recycling bin. Marni combed the house, but the black pumps were gone.

Then it hit her! She'd probably put them in with the items for the charity. *Oh no!* How could she have made such a mistake? She'd intended to give away her old pumps, not her new ones. She sank into a chair. What now? How embarrassing to call the charity office and ask to have them returned. Anyway, they were probably long gone to someone who recognized a great buy at the thrift shop. What a stupid mistake she'd made and what a loss. Marni sat for a few moments, thinking about what she'd done. Then suddenly it came to her. God was in this with her. He must have had a special person in mind for those shoes—someone who really needed a pair just that size. She might never find out who the person was, but she could be sure her new shoes were a blessing to someone. *Thank you, God, for using me in a way I'd never have thought of on my own.*

Today's Thoughts
*So in everything, do to others what
you would have them do to you.*
MATTHEW 7:12

Lord, please help me give to others from my abundance not merely from what I no longer want or need.

Age-Old Challenges

14

Licensed to Age

Pat visited her sister Liz, a resident of Lakeside Retirement Living. Everywhere Pat turned there were reminders of her season of life—gray-haired men, women walking with canes or walkers, emergency pull cords in each room in case of a fall or accident, chair exercise classes, a retirement community bus, a memory-care facility for those with dementia, and prunes on the breakfast buffet."

"Oh dear," she mumbled to herself. "It's that time of life. I never thought I'd actually reach this stage, but here I am. I'm glad to be a visitor, though, and not a resident—at least not yet."

The day after Pat arrived for the weekend she took a long walk on her own. She needed to reassure herself that she could still get around without assistance. She also needed a dose of sunshine and blue sky to keep her from getting down about getting older. As she rounded a corner on her way back to her sister's apartment, she spotted a car with a personalized license plate that read: UR2OLD.

"Excuse me!" Pat said louder than she expected. But her ire was up. "Talk about yourself, you oldster!" she barked at the anonymous person who owned the car. "Don't judge me."

Pat then took a breath and calmed down, mentally editing the letters on the plate to suit herself: UROLD2. If that were her license plate, she'd make a point of parking right next to UR2OLD!

Today's Thoughts

This God is our God for ever and ever;
he will be our guide even to the end.

PSALM 48:14

Thank you, Lord, that age is of no importance to you. I am ageless in your sight. What matters is the state of my soul. May I always walk in your light.

15

My Way or the Highway

Les and Jan enjoy a good wrestling match on TV, but when they resort to wrestling with each other they're not so compatible. In fact, according to Jan, they can get into it over the most trivial issues.

One day they argued about what was the best route to take from their home to their friends' home. The Raymonds lived about twenty minutes away by car. Jan shared, "Les insisted on going the longer way, which adds three to five minutes, depending on traffic conditions." But then Jan admitted their ongoing conflict is less about the route than it is about her idea of what saves time. "His route has stop signs but mine has signals."

Jan confesses to being a risk-taker. "I'm less law-abiding than my husband. In my opinion it's okay to drive over the speed limit in order to race through a yellow light. I hate delays and dislike waiting even more. And what about stop signs? Although I know it's the law to come to a full stop at an intersection, it hardly seems necessary when no one else is even close. 'Brief' stops seem equivalent to rushing through a yellow light to me."

Jan does admit that the route with stop signs is safer than the one with signal lights, where you have to guess whether to speed up or slow down because the light could change at any moment and you don't want to be caught in the middle of the road. That would be a crash for sure.

One day, Jan decided to test out her theory. She headed to the Raymonds' house alone, choosing to take her husband's way. "I wanted to clock it while I was behind the wheel to prove my point once and for all." Because she wasn't tensed up by gauging whether she'd make the lights like she would on her route, Jan found herself daydreaming a bit, suddenly unconcerned about time or speed. "I could see the tortoise and hare scenario playing out before my eyes. The slower way was definitely inching along at a more rapid pace than I'd realized when I was arguing my point with my husband."

And then she noticed his way went alongside the exquisite ocean too. "Had I really been so set on winning my argument and capturing a couple extra minutes that I'd missed the beautiful sea—a view few people get to enjoy while driving? Yes!"

Jan returned home that day a bit chagrined. She apologized to her husband for being argumentative and admitted that the moments she "wasted" while going the longer way were priceless compared to the minutes she would have saved going her way.

Today's Thoughts
The farmer knows just what to do for
God has given him understanding.
Isaiah 28:26 nlt

Thank you, Lord, that when I don't know which way to turn, you point the way. And when I insist on my own way, I'm so glad you still love me and guide me back to your way.

16

Somewhere in the Middle

Louise loved to take long, leisurely walks around the retirement complex where she lived. She was at the age of needing a bit of help though. She always carried her cell phone, but sometimes she forgot her key. It was a good thing the security guards had sets of master keys on their belts at all times. A guard would zip over in a moment when she called to say she was stranded in front of her door.

Occasionally she felt a bit wobbly on her legs, so if she needed assistance taking a shower or dressing, she could call for help. And, of course, it was nice not to have to cook anymore…or clean…or water the lawn. All those chores were taken care of by various members of the staff.

Louise also found it useful to wear an identification tag around her wrist with her name, cottage address, and her son's phone number in case of emergency. Overall, she was now happy and satisfied that this was the place she needed to be. She could live out her remaining days in peace and contentment and enjoy the fellowship of her two neighbors. May lived on the right, and June lived on the left.

One day while out walking, Louise suddenly realized she'd forgotten to put on her ID tag. *Oh well, I'm not going far. I'll just take a short stroll today*, she decided. As she was walking, an older man with a huge black dog passed her on the sidewalk. The dog lunged at Louise, and she jumped back, fell down, and bumped her head. She didn't black out, but she sure felt dizzy for a moment or two.

"Oh, ma'am, I'm so sorry!" The gentleman with the dog gushed his apology as he stood by her side. "I don't know what got into Blackie. He's usually very compliant. Please let me help you."

Louise saw that his dog was sitting quietly now, so she took the man's hand and got to her feet. "I'll be all right. It was just a fright."

"Let me walk you home. I insist. What's your address?"

She hesitated.

The man looked at her and then broke into a smile. "No worries, ma'am. I'm not a kidnapper. I just want to be sure you return to your cottage safely. Please give me your address."

By this time Louise was embarrassed. Finally she muttered, "I can't think of the number, but I live between May and June in the retirement complex around the corner." *Oh dear, he must think I'm off my rocker!* Louise laughed out loud at his funny look. "They're my neighbors," she clarified.

"Ah," the man said. "Since I don't know where May and June live, let's play it safe and stop at the administration office. Someone there will be able to help, I'm sure."

Today's Thoughts

Though he may stumble, he will not fall,
for the LORD *upholds him with his hand.*

PSALM 37:24

I'm glad you're looking out for me, dear God, or who knows what would become of me.

17

Nice Place to Be

Dottie looked forward to her family's visit each Sunday at the retirement complex she lived in. She attended church with them, and then they enjoyed Sunday brunch together, as well as a little visit in the rose garden. This was the highlight of her week.

One Sunday, as Dottie and her family were having a bit of conversation, her friend Jane walked by with Nancy. Jane introduced Nancy to Dottie and the others. Nancy, the outgoing personality that she was, made small talk, commenting on the rose bushes and the color of Dottie's blouse and skirt. She tickled the chin of the baby in Dottie's daughter's arms.

"I'll bet this is your great-grandchild," purred Nancy. "How adorable." She asked the girl's name and then continued adding her two-cents worth to the conversation. Jane elbowed her friend, signaling her to move on, but Nancy didn't take the hint. Finally Jane interrupted and announced that lunch would soon be served so they'd better get moving.

With that Nancy plopped down on the bench beside Dottie and took her small hands in her own. "So nice to meet you, Dottie, and your dear family. I bet your son and daughter-in-law love knowing you are here, safe and sound—the same way I feel about Jane." Nancy gestured to the flowers and trees and stone work in the garden. "This seems to me the perfect place to be this side of heaven."

"Don't push it," Dottie announced. "I'm in no rush to get to heaven. As for this being a nice place to be—well, okay, I'll agree on that too—*if* I have to be in a place."

Today's Thoughts
This is what [Jesus] promised us—eternal life.
1 John 2:25

Thank you, Lord, that you've gone before me and are preparing a place for me with you in heaven.

18

Choosing to Believe

Marti phoned her friend Gretchen to congratulate her on her eighty-fifth birthday. Gretchen didn't seem too happy about reaching that milestone.

"I'd rather forget this day, if you don't mind. Getting old is wearing on me, if you know what I mean. There's one thing and then another to contend with—aching knees, tired eyes, sore toes, pinched nerves. You don't want to head in this direction, Marti. There's no going backward—that's the problem."

Marti, being the positive thinking person she is, couldn't take another earful of Gretchen's negative response. Marti had only called to say "happy birthday" and invite her friend to lunch. But at this rate, she'd give the second part of her idea a second thought. Did she really want to sit down over a salad and listen to Gretchen recite her woes? *On the other hand, poor Gretch is a widow now and unable to enjoy life as she once did. Maybe I'm being selfish. I'll give her another chance.*

"Gretchen, have you heard the latest statistics regarding aging? They are really quite amazing. For example, the experts now say that women who are 60 today are actually more like age 50. So that means at age 85 you're the new 75. How about that? You just bought yourself 10 more years. Congratulations!"

"Don't you believe a word of it!" Gretchen shot back. "Somebody's lying to you. When you reach 85 you'll know what I'm talking about." And with that she said goodbye and hung up.

Marti wouldn't be discouraged that easily. She looked in the mirror and smiled. "Congratulations to me!" she said to her reflection. "When you turn 63 next week you'll be the new 53. Even if it's a lie, I choose to believe it."

Today's Thoughts

Even to your old age and gray hairs
I am he, I am he who will sustain you.

Isaiah 46:4

I may count my life in years, but by your grace, O Lord, I am as young as I feel. Thank you for giving me life.

19

New to Eighty

Sally developed some health concerns following her eightieth birthday. She made an appointment with her doctor, and afterward he scheduled a variety of tests to see what was going on. Two weeks later she returned to his office to review the results.

Doctor Ames studied her file. "How old are you?"

"Eighty," Sally said proudly. "In case you don't know, I'm a dedicated and involved grandmother. I lead an active life, including holding a part-time job. In fact, I've held my position as a receptionist for the last 30 years."

The doctor looked at her again—more intently this time. "How old did you say you are?"

"Eighty." She winked. "I hope you find that hard to believe."

"I do find it hard. You don't look 80. You look amazing—I mean, you look very healthy."

Sally smiled. "Well, being 80 is a new experience. I've only been this age for a few days."

Doctor Ames chuckled and closed Sally's file. "I'm happy to report there is no cause for alarm. You don't have anything to worry about. Aches and pains are age-related and, as you said, 'Being 80 is a new experience.' Happy belated birthday. Come see me again in six months, and we'll see how you're doing with being 80."

Today's Thoughts

Life will be brighter than noonday,
and darkness will become like morning.

Job 11:17

Thank you, Lord, that even in the late years of my life I can triumph over darkness with the light of your love and grace.

20

Not So Easy

Lucille pulled up to the curb in front of Janet's house. It had become their custom to go to church together each Sunday morning. Lucille admired her friend's stamina at age 79. She thought Janet had managed to hang on to her looks, as well. Janet had a lovely complexion, sparkling blue eyes, and a crown of softly curled white hair. In addition, she dressed appropriately for her age. She knew just what parts of her body to conceal and which ones to reveal, which were fewer with each advancing year, as she often admitted.

This particular morning Janet walked out of her home and down the three porch steps on her way to Lucille's car. Lucille noticed how especially pretty Janet appeared in a light-blue pantsuit that matched the color of her eyes. Her fingernails were beautifully manicured as well.

As Janet slid into the passenger seat, Lucille took the opportunity to compliment her friend. "You look absolutely stunning today," she said cheerily.

"Thanks," Janet replied. "It's not so easy anymore."

"Well you make it look easy." With that Lucille pulled into the street. The two friends chuckled a lot as they talked about the effort it took to keep up appearances when their bodies did everything they could to give the women a hard time.

"We just have to fight back," said Lucille.

"I'm with you." Janet pulled out a coupon she'd received from a local spa—a two-for-one price for an entire day's indulgence, including a massage, a facial, and time in the sauna.

The women gave each other high fives and agreed to sign up the very next day.

Today's Thoughts

Walk in obedience to all that the Lord *your God*
has commanded you, so that you may live and
prosper and prolong your days.

Deuteronomy 5:33

Dear God, I welcome the coming years regardless of what they bring because through it all you lead the way.

21

What Day Is It?

Chuck was convinced he was getting old. No question about it. Half the time lately he didn't know what day it was. Monday to Friday seemed to race by with no particular difference between one day and the next.

When he'd been a workingman, it was easy to know which day was which. Mondays were laundry days at his house. His wife, Grace, had the washing machine and dryer spinning all day and part of the evening.

Tuesdays were his lunch dates with the guys in his shop.

On Wednesdays Chuck and Grace hosted an evening Bible study and potluck dinner.

Thursdays were date nights. He and Grace enjoyed their weekly pizza at Hal's, followed by ice cream cones.

And Fridays, well they signaled the end of the workweek, so Chuck never had a problem remembering those days.

But now that Chuck was retired, all the days were a jumble except weekends. He kept track of Saturdays and Sundays because of golf and church. What was he to do to keep track of the rest of the time? He couldn't bear the thought of being an old geezer who was falling by the side of the road.

One afternoon Chuck poured out his woes to his seven-year-old grandson, Lance, as they were going home from the boy's baseball practice. *Maybe Lance will sympathize with me. Grace surely doesn't because she can't stand the idea of being married to an old man.*

Lance wrinkled his brow for a moment after listening to Chuck's lament. Then he brightened. "Grandpa, I have a great idea. Look at your vitamin case on the kitchen table. There's a little section for each day's pills, right?"

Chuck nodded.

"Well, all you have to do is look at the name of the day when you take your vitamins. I'll get you started. Today is Tuesday. When we get back to your house, we'll open the compartment for tomorrow. Wake up in the morning and look at your open vitamin case. You'll see it's Wednesday. You'll never be mixed up again, I promise."

"But what if I forget to take my pills or to open the next little section?"

"Well, Grandpa, that's my best idea. You're on your own if that doesn't work. Mom says we all have to take responsibility for our own actions. Know what I mean?"

Chuck nodded. He sure did.

Today's Thoughts

You, LORD, keep my lamp burning.
PSALM 18:28

Lord, Lance has a point. I need to keep on keeping on till you call me home. Please sharpen my mind and set my will with yours in all things.

22

Bad Hair Day

Martha's bad hair day wasn't due to wind or rain. It started with shampooing. "I love the little containers of shampoo and conditioner you get when you stay overnight in a hotel," said Martha. "They don't contain the additives and fragrances like the name brands I usually buy, and I love how they work on my hair. When my daughter and I go out of town, we always gather up the free samples and take them home."

During one visit, while getting ready to step into the shower, Martha pulled off her glasses, got her towel ready, and placed her cell phone by the tub. She had everything within easy reach. "Then I remembered I needed more conditioner. I grabbed a couple of bottles from the counter and stepped into the shower. I shampooed and rinsed and then reached for the conditioner. A thought hit me: *Did I get the right bottle?* I tried to read the label, but without my glasses all I could see was what appeared to be a long word. 'It must be conditioner,' I decided."

For fear of running out of hot water, Martha quickly shook out a handful from the bottle and rubbed it through her hair. In a matter of seconds her head felt sticky and gooey. She rinsed it immediately, but the more water she used, the worse it got. The water turned lukewarm and then cold.

"What did I put in my hair?" she shouted. Panicking, she grabbed the bottle of shampoo from the shower, finished that one and used another one before she finally had a clean head of hair—and in cold water! She stepped out of the shower and pulled a towel around her to get warm.

She reached for her glasses to see what she'd used. Moisturizing lotion! No wonder it was sticky and gooey. But her hair did feel silky and soft. Not all bad after all.

Today's Thoughts
The Spirit helps us in our weakness.
ROMANS 8:26

Lord, you don't keep me from making big or little mistakes, but you do assure me that you're with me and will guide me through the situation. Thank you for being with me always.

23

Too Hot!

Anita and her mother, Ingrid, chose a cozy booth in their favorite café. They were going to enjoy their monthly lunch together.

Ingrid started the conversation. "We had a wonderful gift fair at church last weekend. You'd be surprised at how much we brought in from the sale of third-world goods. And a neighbor church sold even more of them. It was so exciting to hear about such a good response."

Anita smiled so her mother would know she was interested and paying attention. She commented, "So the total was about $105k?"

"Your temperature is 105!" Ingrid's voice rose. "Oh my! You need a doctor! Honey, you're really sick. Let's go to urgent care right now. I'll drive while you pray." She put down the menu, reached for her car keys, and stood.

"Mom, wait! I'm fine, really. Do you have your hearing aids in?" Anita asked. But she was too late. Ingrid was already hurrying out the door.

Today's Thoughts
*"I will restore you to health and
heal your wounds," declares the LORD.*
JEREMIAH 30:17

God, thank you for giving me the most precious kind
of well-being—a soul redeemed by Christ Jesus.

24

Membership Closed

It was the first day of a long bus trip through Spain. While strolling along a cobblestone walk during the first break, Michelle stumbled, fell, and blacked out. When she came to, she was mortified. Men and women were clustered around. Seeing she was conscious, they kept asking if she wanted to go to the hospital. From the expressions on their faces, they were clearly worried.

"No. No ambulance and no hospital," she stated firmly. "I'll be all right in a moment. I must have slipped on a pebble or something."

"It's those sandals you're wearing," chimed in one of the men standing by her. "Put on some real walking shoes."

Not too sympathetic, Michelle thought. *But he's probably right.* She took his words to heart as she touched her throbbing head and checked out her skinned knees. A nurse on the trip stepped forward and encouraged her to stand up and sip some water. She gave Michelle a going over, checking for a serious head injury and broken bones.

"So far, so lucky," the woman said with a smile. "I think you're in shock more than anything. We'll help you back to the bus so you can rest."

The following day the passengers stepped onto the bus after breakfast and enjoyed a long drive through the countryside before making their next stop at an old castle. Cora slid to the edge of her seat in the front row and stood. As she stepped into the aisle down she went, face forward into the entry well of the bus. The tour guide had put out a steadying hand and kept her from taking a true header. Fortunately, Cora was wearing a wool hat and a raincoat—both helped protect her from serious injury. But she did bonk the side of her head and cut her chin. She noticed her silk scarf had fallen out of her purse and was on the floor. That's what caused her misstep.

On day 4 of the 12-day journey, as tour members went through an old house with a winding staircase, Milton missed the narrow end of one of the descending steps and tumbled forward, crashing into his wife, who was just ahead of him. She was sent flying to the bottom of the stairway. Blood spurted everywhere, spotting the walls, the steps, and the couple's clothing. Within minutes they were whisked off to the emergency room at a nearby hospital. They returned that evening with Milton's head bandaged and his wife's right knee bearing five stitches.

If it weren't so sad it would have been amusing. The next morning when everyone was aboard the bus and accounted for, the tour leader quipped, "Sorry, folks. We've had such a rush of people trying to join 'The Fall Club' that we've had to close the membership."

Everyone laughed, agreed, and for the remaining days of the trip all was well. One oldster quipped, "That's what happens when you get a bunch of seniors together. We keep trying to trip each other up!"

Today's Thoughts

The gracious hand of our God is on
everyone who looks to him.

EZRA 8:22

Lord, how blessed I am that no matter what I do, or where I go, or how many challenges I face, there you are guiding and comforting me and healing my wounds.

25

Charge!

"What happened?" Samantha asked as she sat up in the easy chair. She was sitting in darkness. The lights were out. The TV was off. The fridge was no longer humming. *I must have dozed off,* she decided. She stood and ambled along the wall in the living room to the hallway and then down to her bedroom, afraid of falling with no light to guide her. Even the small nightlights were out.

She suddenly realized she hadn't charged her mobile phone for a few days. If her daughter tried to call, she wanted to be sure she could get through. Samantha fumbled in a drawer for a flashlight, found one, and flicked it on. She scurried back down the hallway to the countertop where she kept her phone. Quickly she hooked the phone to the charger and plugged it into the wall socket. Nothing happened.

"Oh, no! What's next?" she muttered. Then it hit her. If the lights were out, the television was off, and the entire house was pitch-black, obviously the electricity was off so why did she think she could charge her phone? *Ah! Another one of those senior moments.*

Samantha felt her way back to her easy chair, sat down, pulled a blanket tightly around her lap and shoulders, and slipped off to sleep. *It will be light soon enough,* she consoled herself. And sure enough it was. When she awakened, the TV was on and the lights too. Now she didn't need lamplight. It was morning and the sun was peeking through her kitchen window. And best of all, the fridge was humming again. Time for breakfast, time to reset all the clocks, time to charge her phone. The power outage was over.

Today's Thoughts

When Jesus spoke again to the people, he said,
"I am the light of the world.
Whoever follows me will never walk in
darkness, but will have the light of life."

JOHN 8:12

Lord, how good to be reassured that when I think the lights have gone out in my life, you are with me to restore them. You are the light of the world. When I walk with you, I have all the light I need.

26

The Perils of Smoking

"Hi, Mom!" Rory said after answering the phone. She raised the volume of her voice as well as she could considering her sore throat and cough. She felt miserable, but she didn't want to discourage her mother by cutting the conversation short. Rory knew it was an effort for her mother to make phone calls.

"What's going on over there?" her mom asked. "You sound so far away."

"I have a cold. And to make matters worse, Richard just put a special log in the woodstove today to burn out the creosote that can stop up the chimney. If we don't take care of it now, it's likely the smoke from the stove will back up and fill the room eventually. That would be all I need at this point. How about you? I hope you're doing better than I am."

Rory's mother cleared her throat and exclaimed, "What? You let guests smoke in your house?"

Oh dear! Rory started the explanation all over again, but her voice had collapsed so she coughed between each word.

"Oh dear!" her mother shouted. "Are you all right? You should have known better after all these years. *Never ever let anyone smoke in your house!* You are allergic to smoke. You always have been. What were you thinking?"

"Mom! I wasn't…"

"See what I mean? You weren't thinking! I knew it. Well, you tell your guests to put out their cigarettes right now or leave immediately. And you can tell them your mother said so!"

Rory gave up. "Sure thing, Mom. Great advice. I'll call you tomorrow."

Today's Thoughts

I was sick and you looked after me.

MATTHEW 25:36

There are many ways to be sick—but no matter the way, you are here to comfort and heal me. Thank you, Lord.

27

Oh, No!

Sandy plucked her phone out of her purse and called her friend Marie. The two had talked about sharing information for a project they were working on for a club they both belonged to. Sandy wanted to recommend a book for Marie to read. After sharing about the book, Sandy said, "Hang on! It's in the living room. I'll put down the phone for just a second and get it. I'll be right back."

Sandy laid the phone on the kitchen table, went into the living room, and reached for the book on a shelf above the fireplace. With book in hand, she grabbed her phone and chatted away, giving Marie the title of the book and a few other details related to their project.

But Marie didn't respond. She didn't even say, "No thanks," or "good idea," or "nice of you to think of me."

"Marie, are you there? What's going on?" Sandy said. She felt her face flush with frustration. Still no reply from Marie. Sandy held her phone out and looked at it. That's when she realized she'd picked up the small clock on the coffee table—not her cell phone that she'd left in the kitchen!

Oh, no! By now Marie is probably wondering what happened to me! Just then her cell phone chimed. Sandy went into the kitchen, picked it up, and glanced at the face. Sure enough, it was Marie calling.

Sandy had some explaining to do, including apologizing for the mistake and for her thoughts when she was sure Marie was being rude.

"I heard your voice fading away," said Marie, "and then I didn't hear it anymore. I finally hung up."

The two friends had a really good laugh and admitted that getting old certainly has its hang-ups.

Today's Thoughts

[God] will yet fill your mouth with laughter and
your lips with shouts of joy.

JOB 8:21

A good belly laugh is such good medicine when I find myself in ridiculous predicaments. Once I let it out, I can go on with a smile. Lord, thank you for giving me a sense of humor.

At Play

28

A Small World

Rosemary was fed up with Genevieve, one of her tablemates in the dining room of Wellington Senior Living. Rosemary had moved in just six months before and quickly discovered Genevieve simply wouldn't stop talking about her many travels to this continent and that, up one river and down another, and over sea and mountain. It seemed there was barely a speck on the globe that she and her husband hadn't explored.

Today it was all Rosemary could do to hold her tongue. She and Abner, her husband, had done very little traveling. They were homebodies, content with their life as it was—until recently. When their big house became too much for them, they moved to Wellington.

Genevieve and Walter could no longer travel due to his declining health, but that didn't stop Genevieve from blabbing about all they'd done back in the day. She seemed to be challenging everyone at the table to match or outdo what she and her husband had accomplished in their 52 years of marriage.

"Well," Genevieve asked Rosemary one day at breakfast, "wasn't life boring just staying put? Never enlarging your circle, learning about the world and other cultures, and finding out how other people live? I can't imagine it."

"Oh, we did travel," Rosemary corrected, biting back the sarcasm she wanted to drop in Genevieve's lap. "We preferred to take short trips to interesting places that enriched our lives."

Genevieve set down her coffee cup. "Really? You've never

mentioned that. What kind of trips? Where did you go? I bet Walter and I have been to some of the same spots. Short trips, you said?"

"Yes, very short. And I'm certain you've been there too. In fact, I've seen you at some of the places."

"Tell me more!" Genevieve was all ears.

"Short trips…to Save-a-lot Pharmacy, Minnie's Flower Shop, Doctor Benson's office, and Gas for Less Fuel." Rosemary smiled as she picked up her cup and took a sip. She eyed her tablemate over the rim.

At last Genevieve was speechless!

Today's Thoughts

Like a north wind that brings unexpected rain is
a sly tongue—which provokes a horrified look.

PROVERBS 25:23

Lord, sometimes it's really difficult to listen when other people go on and on about their lives with little thought or comment about mine. Help me be quick to listen and slow to judge.

29

Dad's Turn

Saturday morning Tom pulled out his old pup tent, the hiking poles he hadn't seen in a decade, and the cookstove and backpack he'd used umpty-ump years ago when he was a young man and his two sons were little. *Where did the time go?* he wondered. *I was strong then, and they were fragile. Now I'm fragile, and they're strong.*

He looked through his pantry. Not much there but a few cans of soup and chili. The fridge held some wilted lettuce, a carton of milk, and a loaf of stale bread. Ever since his wife had passed away six months before, Tom had lost interest in food...make that life. He felt depressed a lot of the time, and he couldn't muster the energy to do the things he once did with such vigor.

Now the boys wanted him to go on a camping trip with them. Tom didn't want to disappoint them, but he also couldn't picture himself tromping up the side of a mountain or holding out on a trail for hours at a time. He shook his head. He'd have to decline. That was that.

The front door opened, and in walked Rich and Hal.

"Dad, we've come to give you a hand," said Rich. "We're leaving Monday, don't forget. We'll need a couple of hours today to make sure you have everything you need."

Tom's stomach soured. How could he tell the boys he wasn't going? They seemed so excited for this father and sons excursion.

Hal was carrying a huge bag and a box. He set them down on the living room floor. "Rich and I got these for you, Dad. Take a look."

Tom's eyes flooded. It wasn't even his birthday, and yet here was a load of gifts! He lifted the lid on the box. New hiking boots—just his size. He opened the big bag and inside was the latest model backpack, complete with pockets for everything from a carving knife to a camera, from a bottle of water to snacks.

"You boys thought of everything, didn't you? I don't know what to say."

"No words necessary." Hal clapped his dad on the back. "The backpack is for your personal items, Dad. Rich and I will handle the tent, sleeping bags, stove, and food."

Tom pulled out a handkerchief from his back pocket and wiped his eyes. "Thank you so much. I'll be ready bright and early Monday morning!"

"Our pleasure, Dad," Rich said. "It's your turn to get to depend on us just like we depended on you 25 years ago when you took us hiking."

Today's Thoughts
All the believers…broke bread in their homes and
ate together with glad and sincere hearts, praising God.
ACTS 2:44,46-47

O Lord, thank you for my family and friends. They make life so interesting. Help me to share your love and care with them. Give me opportunities to talk about you.

30

Weather Rewind

Donna and Jack were high school sweethearts. They've now been married some 48 years and enjoy a full life. Jack likes to work long hours, and Donna is a writer and speaker, so they don't have a lot of free time for one another. They do enjoy each other's company when they get together though.

Like many older couples, they like to watch a good movie in the evening after dinner. Staying awake till the end is another matter. After working hard all day, it's pretty common for one or both to nod off and lose track of the plot.

One Thursday evening they sat down to watch a fast-paced action thriller. Midway through the film Jack sat up in his recliner. "Donna, do you know what just happened?"

Donna yawned. "I don't have a clue. Go ahead and rewind it. I'll pay more attention this time."

By the end of the movie they looked at each other with puzzled expressions. They still didn't have a clue what the plot was.

"What was that about?" Jack asked.

"I can't say," Donna said, shaking her head. "Rewind."

After the second go-round, Jack switched channels to the local weather.

Donna shook her head. "What did he just say? I missed it."

Jack looked at his wife with a grin. "It's pretty sad when we even have to rewind the weather!"

Today's Thoughts
When you lie down, your sleep will be sweet.
PROVERBS 3:24

Lord, it's good to know that you're with me day and night, whether I'm awake or asleep. Your everlasting arms are always around me.

31

Window Shopping

One Saturday morning Barney set out to do some repairs around the house and garage. He'd put them off for too long. He made a list and checked it twice. Then he ran it by his wife, Lola. Lola was not one for leaving Barney in charge. He was bound to forget something important, she was sure.

Barney knew Lola enjoyed reminding him in no uncertain terms of what he'd forgotten. He backed out of the driveway, list in hand, and blew a kiss to his wife.

She threw one back and waved. "Have fun and don't spend too much," she shouted— the same advice she'd given him for the past 40 years.

Barney scratched his head. How can a man have fun and, at the same time, not spend too much? Buying stuff was one of his few pleasures in these later years. He loved gizmos and gadgets.

Lola did have one weakness. She liked to be surprised every now and then with a bunch of daisies or a bottle of sparkling grape juice. He decided he'd give that some thought while he was in town. It was always good to keep the little woman on his side.

Barney roamed the aisles of Dunton's Hardware and then strolled through O'Reilly's Auto Parts store. There was always something new and exciting to look at…and buy. But today he had to get down to business and get supplies to repair the broken shutter. He was also going to replace the garage window he'd cracked when he knocked the rake against it last spring. Lola would be so pleased when she could cross this chore off her honey-do list. Barney returned home with the glass and tools he needed.

When he walked into the house, Lola greeted him with a hug and kiss and a twinkle in her eye. "How did it go?" she asked.

Is she hinting at something? Barney wondered. He couldn't read her mind, and he wished she'd just speak up. He did feel a vague sense that he'd left something out. Suddenly he remembered he'd forgotten to pick up the bottle of juice and the bunch of flowers. He hit his forehead with a palm. Rats!

He looked up. Lola was waiting for an answer. "It went fine," Barney said. "I know you'll be happy to hear that I did a little window shopping."

"Window shopping for two hours?"

"Yep! Window shopping. I bought a new piece of glass to replace the garage window." *That ought to bring a smile*, he thought.

"Anything else?" she asked.

Barney saw the hopeful look in her eyes. He did some quick thinking. "Nothing you need to know about…yet."

Lola threw her arms around him and kissed him on the cheek.

Barney hugged her back and then headed out to the garage. First things first! He whipped out his phone and called Beacon Dinner House. He made reservations for two. *This might even lead to a sweet kiss!* he decided. Now he was in the mood to fix that window.

Today's Thoughts

My chosen ones will long enjoy the works of their hands.
ISAIAH 65:22

Lord, thank you for giving me the time and skills to maintain my home and my relationships.

32

Turtle Race

Minnie wanted to liven things up a bit at Meadowbrook Senior Living where she'd recently moved. She loved the array of activities to choose from to fill her days, but they were too tame. Croquet? Bridge? Flower arranging? *Pul-eeze!* There had to be more available than those ordinary pastimes. She wanted to join hiking and running groups, but at 86 she knew those days were over. Still, she was committed to staying active. Minnie decided to organize a day of sports for the residents—offering a variety of suitable activities.

She came up with a plan and presented it to Miss Marston, the recreation manager, for consideration. Minnie's suggestions included exercises that everyone could participate in—even those who relied on wheelchairs and walkers.

Miss Marston looked over the well-written proposal and was about to give her stamp of approval when she noticed something called "Turtle Race."

"I'm sorry," she said. "This is one activity that will have to go. We can't have live turtles running around our recreation room. Let's come up with an alternative."

Minnie pushed back with logic of her own. "But, Miss Marston, we can't eliminate that one. I think it will be one of the highlights. People will love it. And we'll have prizes for the winners."

"I'm afraid not." Miss Marston was adamant. "No turtles, and that's that. I'm sorry."

Minnie wouldn't take no for an answer. She admitted with a

smile, "Okay, I have a confession. The kind of turtles *I'm* talking about are no trouble at all." A sheepish grin crossed her face. "I'm proposing a *walking people* race. People walking at a turtle's pace. The residents will do the racing, and the first and last ones will win pet turtles."

Today's Thoughts

*"Make level paths for your feet," so that the lame
may not be disabled, but rather healed.*
HEBREWS 12:13

I may not be able to run as fast as I once did, but you make my paths straight, Lord. You strengthen my legs so that I won't be set aside in the race for your kingdom.

33

Front to Back

The Roberts clan gathered for a backyard barbecue to honor Grandpa Lou on his birthday. Lou's wife, Rosemarie, was very excited about donning her brand-new, white Capri pants and coral-colored top, which she'd bought for the occasion. She wanted to show off her new figure after losing a few pounds.

She pulled on the pants and slipped the long top over her head, pulling it snugly around her hips. Then she touched up her makeup and hair. She was ready when the family arrived. While walking back and forth from the kitchen to the yard, she felt the pants tug. *That's a bit odd,* she thought. Sitting was also uncomfortable, but still, it was a small price to pay for the wonderful way she felt without the extra five pounds she'd been trying to shed for so long. Maybe she'd picked up the wrong size of pants by mistake. She'd handle it on Monday. Now was the time to enter into the spirit of the birthday celebration! After the meal, Rosemarie went into the guest bathroom to loosen her pants a bit after that extra helping of barbecued ribs. She discovered to her surprise that she'd put the pants on backward! The back patch pockets were in the front. *Good thing the pants had an elastic waistband!*

Before switching them around, she decided to give everyone a good laugh. She walked into the kitchen where the family had gathered to clean up and showed them what she'd done. Everyone laughed and congratulated her on being willing to admit her mistake.

Six-year-old Benny, however, stole the spotlight from his grand-mother. "As long as your head is screwed on the right way, Grandma. That's all that matters at your age."

Today's Thoughts
They will still bear fruit in old age,
they will stay fresh and green.
PSALM 92:14

Yes, Lord, I want to continue to bear fruit! Help me keep my mind steady and alert. Let me retain my sense of humor even when people have a bit of fun at my expense.

34

Duck Hunting

Rudy and his dad, Will, took to the woods for a day of duck hunting. They had a high old time chasing the ducks, stopping for lunch by a stream, and then taking up their sport again. When they reached the legal limit of ducks taken, they headed back to Rudy's truck.

The trek involved crossing a stream, so Rudy led the way. Both men were wearing their chest-high waders so they could stay dry. Rudy turned at one point to check on his dad—to make sure he was okay and keeping pace. But all he saw were two hands straight up in the air—one clutching the pouch with the ducks (protecting them from getting wet?) and the other holding his shotgun. Then the rest of his dad surfaced. He'd evidently slipped on the river rocks. Rudy rushed back to his dad.

Will stood up and said he was fine.

They had a good laugh over the fact that Will was so intent on protecting his catch and his weapon that he'd never given a thought about trying to cushion his fall to the river bottom. Thankfully he wasn't hurt.

The two men then drove home to tell the womenfolk.

Today's Thoughts
Though I sit in darkness, the LORD will be my light.
MICAH 7:8

Dear God, I don't own a gun and I don't hunt, but I can relate to this story because sometimes I am so intent on holding on to what's unimportant that I neglect to pay attention to what is.

35

Fire!

Susan looked forward to a little romance with her new husband, Fred. She'd been a widow for 10 years, so she considered having a spouse after so long a special gift from God. The couple had been married a month, and Susan wanted to mark the occasion with a lovely dinner, beautiful music on the stereo, and an intimate evening sitting in front of the fireplace in their new townhouse.

That evening Fred walked in with a bouquet of flowers and a big "Happy Anniversary" balloon. The couple hugged and kissed, and then Susan led her husband to the table decorated with ribbons, candles, and their best china.

Over dinner they enjoyed reminiscing about the day they'd met while sailing on San Diego Bay with a seniors group. Fred took Susan's hand. "The moment I saw you my breath caught. I knew I had to get to know you better."

Susan's face warmed. "I felt the same way. I could tell just looking at you that you were a kind and gentle man—someone I'd been waiting for."

They finished their dinner and carried the apple tarts for dessert over to the sofa in front of the fireplace. Susan poured coffee, and Fred settled back against a flowered pillow. A box of firewood Susan had purchased at the store sat on the platform to the side of the fireplace. Susan opened the screen to place a log on top of the grate, but she was suddenly aware of a glass plate blocking off the fireplace interior. "I don't understand," she said, looking to Fred. "I've never seen a fireplace like this. What's the secret formula for opening this door to build a fire?"

"No formula," he said, grinning. "See that button on the wall? Press it."

Susan did so, and suddenly the logs on the grate burst into flames! She stepped back and stared at the fire.

"It's a gas fireplace," Fred announced. "The logs are fake. Isn't that cool...or rather hot? No need for firewood or matches, and no ashes to clean up!"

Susan looked at the box of logs she'd bought. "How embarrassing!" she said. "I didn't realize..."

"No problem," Fred said, interrupting her. He took his wife's hand. "I don't need wood, or matches, or logs, or twigs, or anything else to keep me warm. *You* light my fire!"

Today's Thoughts
Love one another deeply, from the heart.
1 PETER 1:22

Lord, may my love for others follow your lead of first loving me. You are my example and inspiration.

36

Still Alive and Kickin'

Sam pulled out his camping gear from some years ago. His tent was still in good condition. He had a mattress and sleeping bag, a lantern, a canteen, and a small stove, along with accessories for cooking. A quick trip to the grocery store, and he'd be all set. Now all he needed was a buddy to accompany him.

He called Russ. "What do you say, Russ? Want to go camping for a few days at Lake Dorothy? It's not too far, and the weather there is about perfect this time of year. I have a tent that'll hold the two of us. What can go wrong?"

"Everything!" Russ said pessimistically. "I'm not sure I have roughing it in me anymore."

"What do you mean?" Sam asked, his disappointment evident. The two had camped, and hiked, and rock-climbed together for decades. *Why the sudden hesitancy?* he wondered.

"What if we're swarmed by ants or a snake attacks?" Russ asked.

"You've seen snakes. What's the big deal?"

"A rainstorm could take out the tent. Then what would we do?"

"We'd pack up and go to a motel or drive home."

"Mosquitoes. I'm allergic to insect bites."

"Bring repellant—no problem," Sam countered.

"I'm not sure I can handle camp food at this age."

"Then bring the real thing, and we'll cook to your specifications."

"I'm not as agile as I once was. I might slip and fall—and die on the spot."

"Sure, but that could happen at the grocery store." Sam had had enough of Russ' negativity. "Look, friend," he said, making his case one last time, "you either say yes or no. That's it. Anything can happen at any time. You are going to die one day. Who cares where?"

Russ laughed. "Well, okay, when you put it that way, I might as well say yes. But I'm going to update my will before we go."

"Be sure to include me!" Sam grinned, and his voice revealed his good humor. "I'll be the one who has to carry you home if you die on the trail."

Today's Thoughts

Do not be afraid of those who kill the body
but cannot kill the soul.

MATTHEW 10:28

Lord, isn't it interesting and even humorous the way people worry about this and that when the truth is that if we walk with you we are protected in every way? I'm thankful that you will call me to my heavenly home at just the right time—your time.

Aren't They Grand?

37

It's Not What It Looks Like

Grandma Dee had a good heart and a strong commitment to keeping the community clean and presentable. She took a long walk every day armed with a trash bag so she could pick up stray cans, bits of paper, and empty bottles people tossed aside or the wind blew in. Sometimes she invited a neighbor to join her. Two are better than one, she believed. They could collect twice as much trash, as well. One day Grandma Dee knocked on Trisha's door and invited her to join her on a walk. "Think you can keep up?" she teased. "I move pretty fast for an old lady."

"I'll give it a try, but have pity on a 40-year-old," Trisha teased back. "Keep checking on me just in case I drop behind."

Grandma Dee wasn't too far off the mark when she challenged Trisha, who later admitted she returned from the adventure tired and breathless. The pace and the weight of the clutter she'd collected in her trash bag during the three-mile walk wore her out.

Trisha and Grandma pushed through the gate to Trisha's backyard. Jay, Trisha's teenaged son, met them and offered to lend a hand. He eyed the bags overflowing with empty beer cans, empty candy wrappers, and empty cigarette cartons. He raised an eyebrow. "Did you two have a good time?"

Today's Thoughts

If they obey and serve [God],
they will spend the rest of their days in prosperity
and their years in contentment.

JOB 36:11

A little humor goes a long way when I'm tired and cranky. Thank you, God, for perspective and guidance.

38

Who's Older?

Jean, her daughter Cindy, and her four-year-old granddaughter, Heather, walked into the clothing store in town. Jean was going to buy a new dress for a dinner dance. Because she hadn't purchased a fancy outfit in years, she wanted Cindy's input on what to choose. Jean and her husband, Phil, lived in the country so they spent most of their time farming and caring for their animals.

"Look at this one, Grandma!" called Heather as she fingered the lace and sequins on a long, black number.

Jean took a closer look but shook her head. "Thanks, honey, but I think I'm a bit too old for that style. My arms aren't the greatest anymore. I need a dress with sleeves to cover my wrinkles. I don't think a slit up the skirt is right for me either. I wouldn't want the veins on my legs to show." She touched the dress and sighed. "There was a time, though, when I could have worn such a dress." Jean nodded in her daughter's direction. "It would look great on your mom. She still has pretty arms and legs."

"But she has wrinkles too," Heather said, frowning. "I saw them when she was taking a shower."

"Heather!" Cindy said, having overheard. "Were you spying on me when I wasn't looking?"

"I'm sorry." The young girl hung her head.

Cindy slipped an arm around her daughter's shoulders. "It's all right. I'm your mom! But I didn't know you'd be telling Grandma I'm looking old. I don't have that many wrinkles, do I?"

"No. Grandma has more. Does that mean she's older than you?"

"Definitely! She's *my* mom. Moms come first."

"When will you be as old as Grandma?"

"When you're as old as I am."

Jean quickly changed the subject before Cindy became depressed. "I found a dress!" she exclaimed. "Come and see it!"

Today's Thoughts

You have been my hope, Sovereign LORD,
my confidence since my youth.

PSALM 71:5

I'm so glad I can turn to you, dear God, as the years pass by or I would feel down about the changes and losses that go with aging. You, Lord, are eternal! And you've given me the gift of eternal life, for which I profoundly thank you.

39

Making a Mess

Bonnie and her six-year-old granddaughter, Wendy, assembled the ingredients for their afternoon of baking. Flour, sugar, butter, chocolate chips, baking powder, salt, walnuts, and frosting mix. What fun! Bonnie loved having a few hours with this sweet little girl. They always had a good time turning out a delightful dessert, which they shared with Wendy's family and Bonnie's neighbors. Today it would be several batches of cookies…and maybe some fudge with walnuts.

Bonnie glanced at the clock on the oven: 3:10. They'd better get busy or they wouldn't be finished by dinnertime. She turned to Wendy. "How about you take out the mixing bowls and find the wooden spatula? I'll get the measuring cups and spoons."

"Got it, Grandma!" Wendy got busy with her task. The phone rang, and Bonnie stepped out of the room to answer it.

A loud crash interrupted the call. Bonnie dashed into the kitchen. "What's going on in here? Need some help?" She surveyed her crying granddaughter and the disaster on the tile floor and let out a deep sigh.

"I'm so sorry, Grandma!" Wendy wiped her eyes with the back of her hands. "I was trying to take out the big bowl from underneath the little bowls, and they all fell."

Bonnie took her granddaughter into her arms and patted her blond hair. "It's okay. They're just things. We can always buy more."

"But I made a terrible mess," Wendy said. "Now we can't make our cookies and fudge—and it's all my fault."

Bonnie placed her hands on the little girl's shoulders and knelt down in front of her. "It's really okay with me, honey. And it's okay with God too. He knows we all make mistakes and messes, and he's here to help us clean them up."

Wendy's eyes brightened. "I get it." She smiled. "I remember when you told me that God wants us to make a mess with his love by spreading it all around to everyone we meet."

"That's it exactly," Bonnie responded. "Now let's go to the store and buy a new set of mixing bowls. We've got some baking and loving to do!"

Today's Thoughts

The LORD is good, a refuge in times of trouble.
He cares for those who trust in him.
NAHUM 1:7

Thank you, Lord, that no matter how big a mess I make you are here to help me clean it up. How blessed I am to be called your child.

40

Save, Save, Save

Judy and Wayne devoted themselves to saving everything they could for their children and grandchildren's future. "We've also saved on our spending by using coupons," said Judy.

"Pretty soon I realized Wayne had gone too far!" shared Judy. "One day I noticed his bottle of Head and Shoulders shampoo was empty, so I tossed it into the trash and replaced it with a new one."

The following day when Judy was cleaning the bathtub, the empty shampoo bottle fell into the tub. *How strange!* she thought. Instead of making a fuss, she simply tossed it out once again and placed the new bottle in a prominent place. *Hint! Hint!*

To Judy's surprise, the next day the empty shampoo container was back in the shower. "Look, Wayne," she said to her husband, "it's time to move on. There's no more shampoo in that old bottle. The garbage truck will be coming by tomorrow, so this is the perfect time to toss it out."

"But, Judy, we should save it," Wayne replied. "Maybe the kids can use it for something we haven't thought of."

Judy sighed and then laughed. "One empty shampoo bottle is not going to save the world or add one whit to our children's lives. Enough is enough even when it comes to saving for future generations."

Today's Thoughts
The desires of the diligent are fully satisfied.
PROVERBS 13:4

I'm looking at diligence, dear God. Sometimes I go overboard and slip into obsession. Keep me focused on you, and help me keep my life in balance.

41

Grandpets

Lillian was a busybody—no question about it. The entire senior community was her domain. Some people referred to her as the "mayor of Harmony Retirement Living" because she made everyone's business her business. She tracked who died, who was married to whom, which houses were for sale and for how much, and almost everything else. She took charge of the social committee, heading up Bingo Night, the Thanksgiving Potluck, Movie Sunday, and the Summer Barbecue.

She also had a lot to say about people's decorating schemes (or lack thereof), the exterior paint color of the houses, and the landscaping. And when it came to garden art, signs on fences and garage doors, or any other bits of artistic endeavors, Lillian couldn't hold her tongue.

She nearly met her match when she came up against Roberta, who lived around the corner from her.

The women collided one afternoon when Lillian was walking her little dog, Rowdy, past Roberta's house. Rowdy got loose and jumped up against Roberta, causing her to drop the bag of groceries she was carrying. After helping clean up the spilled cans and boxes, Lillian looked up at Roberta's house and noticed a new sign on the wall by the front window: *Grandpets Welcome Here.*

Lillian blurted out her opinion. "Well, *that* sign doesn't belong on your house. You don't even own a pet."

"My grandchildren are my pets," Roberta replied. "They're soft and cuddly, and they keep me company."

Lillian picked up Rowdy and stroked his back. "Well, I'll be," she retorted. "That's the most foolish thing I've heard today. You should put up a sign that says "Grandkids Welcome Here" since that's what you have."

Roberta flashed a smile. "But that goes without saying. My door is *always* open to my grands."

Today's Thoughts
[The LORD] mocks proud mockers but
shows favor to the humble and oppressed.
PROVERBS 3:34

It's hard to swallow people's unsolicited commentary and advice. Lord, help me practice patience and keep the peace. I want to represent *your* point of view rather than blurting out my own in situations that really get my goat.

42

I Won't Tell...

Loretta looked in the mirror and parted her hair with her fingers. Oops! She was behind schedule for a dye job. The gray roots were starting to show. She didn't want her husband and daughter to remind her that she was getting older. Loretta decided she would call and make an appointment today.

Just then her four-year-old granddaughter, Katie, walked into the bathroom and stared at her. "What are you doing, Grammie?"

Startled, Loretta picked up a hairbrush. "Brushing my hair."

"You look like Kippy. He has brown and white hair too."

Loretta wrinkled her brow. "Who's Kippy?"

"Joanie's dog. He has mostly white with a little bit of brown. But you have mostly brown with a little bit of white, right?"

"Well..."

"It's okay, Grammie. I asked Mommy, and she said underneath you have white hair but you don't like anyone to know. I promise I won't tell anyone—unless they ask. Then I have to tell the truth 'cause it's wrong to tell a lie."

Grammie smiled and said, "Let's hope no one asks!"

"If someone does, I'll just say you're old, and then they can figure it out for themselves," Katie said.

Today's Thoughts

*Gray hair is a crown of splendor; it is
attained in the way of righteousness.*

PROVERBS 16:31

I don't have to play guessing games with you, Lord, or
try to fool you away from the truth. You know every
hair on my head—and its true color—because you
made me.

43

Humor Helps

Marylynn and her teenaged grandson, Ben, were involved in a spirited game of 500 Rummy. Tension grew as they came down the homestretch. Grandma checked the score sheet that Ben had taken charge of. The score was 395 to 325, Ben's favor. He'd won the last time they'd played too, so Marylynn was feeling discouraged. The boy seemed to have passed her up in every way—in height and weight, in knowledge of what was going on in the world, and now in her favorite card game. Her competitive nature was taking a bruising.

Suddenly during what was surely going to be the final hand in this knock-down, drag-out fight for victory, the lights went out, the clocks stopped, and the fridge no longer hummed in the background. What a spooky scene it was.

"No worries," Ben said. "There's a full moon out tonight. We won't be in total darkness."

Marylynn could tell her grandson was trying to comfort her. Then she realized she'd better change the batteries in her clock on the mantle so they wouldn't lose track of the time. She excused herself and fumbled her way into the kitchen for fresh batteries.

Ben came up behind her and put a hand on her shoulder. "Grandma, I hate to be the one to break the news, but when there's a power failure battery-operated machines aren't affected. Putting new batteries in the cordless clock won't make a difference."

Marylynn was certain her face had turned red, and she was glad

Ben couldn't see it in the dark. "What was I thinking?" she said. "Ben, you are so smart. You even know that when the power goes off batteries keep working. What will you teach me next?"

The two had a good laugh and then pulled out some candles so they could finish their card game.

Today's Thoughts

Trust in the LORD with all your heart and
lean not on your own understanding.

PROVERBS 3:5

Sure enough, when I lean on my human mind instead of trusting you with all my heart, I fail. Help me, Lord, to be quick to turn from my limited knowledge and trust your infinite wisdom.

44

Bowled Over

Luke pored through the contents of the attic in his grandfather's house. Now that the elderly man had passed on to heaven, Luke knew it would be all right for him to enjoy some of the things his grandfather had left behind. His granddad had given him permission in a letter Luke received on his previous birthday. "Take what you like and sell or give away the rest…"

On this particular day, Luke was ready to sort through the remaining items to see which ones he wanted to take home. An old shirt caught his attention. It would be more of a keepsake than something to wear. The cuffs were frayed at the edges, but when Luke held it up he detected a hint of his grandpa's fragrance—sweet and warm. He set aside the shirt and dug a little deeper. There was an old birthday card from Grandma to Grandpa on his seventy-fifth birthday and a book of poems. *Nice!*

At the bottom of a trunk in the corner was an old leather bag. He picked it up. Man, it was heavy. Attached to the outside was a tiny photo of Grandpa's face. *I wonder what this is all about*, Luke thought. He unzipped the case. Inside was a gold-flecked bowling ball. What a surprise! Luke laughed out loud. "Wow, Grandpa! I forgot about all those years you bowled on the church league. Cool!"

Luke picked up the ball and fit his thumb and fingers into the holes. He grasped it with both hands. A good, hefty ball that still had some life. What would the guys at work think of this antique? Well, no time like the present to show this off. Maybe he'd even find a league to join in memory of his dear grandfather who had been a pal, a friend, and a good bowler in his day.

Today's Thoughts

I recommend having fun, because there is nothing better for people in this world than to eat, drink, and enjoy life. That way they will experience some happiness along with all the hard work God gives them.

ECCLESIASTES 8:15 NLT

Lord, thank you for work *and* for play. May I live a balanced life for your glory.

45

Clever Guy

Six-year-old Tommy pulled down the photo albums from the bottom shelf of the bookcase in his grandmother's den. He liked to look through them whenever he was bored with TV or video games. He thumbed through the pages while his Grandmother Ann looked on from the desk where she was filing some paperwork. "Gram, can you help me find the pictures of my mom and Uncle Wes and Aunt Chris when they were kids?"

Ann walked over and picked up the burgundy album. She handed it to Tommy. "I think most of their school pictures are in here."

Tommy plopped back on the floor and turned the pages. Each picture was marked with the grade the child was in at the time of the photo. He knew his mom's by heart. There were nine photos of her—from kindergarten to eighth grade. He counted the ones for Aunt Chris too. They were all there. Then he counted the pictures of Uncle Wes. One was missing. There were only eight pictures.

"Gram, what happened to Uncle Wes? There's no picture of him for fifth grade. How weird."

"It's so long ago I don't remember," she said. "We'll have to ask him."

"I don't think we should."

"Why not?"

"He might get embarrassed."

"Really? Why do you think that?"

"Because if he didn't have a picture taken, maybe he never went to school for fifth grade. Maybe he skipped school and doesn't want anyone to know it."

Today's Thoughts

*A person's wisdom brightens their face and
changes its hard appearance.*

ECCLESIASTES 8:1

Dear Lord, kids do say the oddest things. And I'm so glad they do. Their cute comments and unique questions keep me on my toes. I want to stay alert and active as I grow older.

46

Still Together!

Grandma Frances sliced the pizza and set the pan on the dining-room table while the grandkids, Mickey and Melanie, chose a couple of board games to play. Grandpa Jess poured soda and put out napkins and paper plates.

"Let the celebration begin!" shouted Mickey. "I'm glad you invited us over for your anniversary."

"How long have you been married?" Melanie asked as she glanced at the photo of her grandparents' wedding day on the mantel.

"Thirty-nine years," Frances replied without hesitation. "I met Grandpa when I was 17, and we married when I was 18. Such a long time ago." She sighed.

Jess chimed in. "Yep, a long time ago. I remember telling your grandma that I would love her forever and ever. Of course, forever seems pretty huge when you're a teen like I was. I was 19, and we'd barely graduated from high school and then we were a married couple. I told Grandma we'd grow old together."

Mickey piped up. "Well, Grandma and Grandpa, congratulations! You reached your goal."

"What goal?" Melanie frowned.

"Growing old together," said Mickey. "They made it. Look at them. They're old, and they did it together. Way to go, guys!"

He and Grandpa traded high-fives as Grandma laughed. "We did indeed!" she declared.

Today's Thoughts

Each individual among you also is to
love his own wife even as himself,
and the wife must see to it that
she respects her husband.

EPHESIANS 5:33 NASB

Thank you, Lord, that I am growing old with you at my side!

Sweets for
the Sweet

47

A Life Saver

Roger had a sweet tooth, and he assumed everyone else did too. He delighted in bringing candy to the workers at the rescue mission where he volunteered his time. His generosity, however, was a step toward obesity for some of the women who worked at the compound.

One disciplined soul named Rita asked Roger for a favor. "Roger, please bring fruit instead of candy. We're getting too fat munching on all this chocolate and caramel, and they're bad for our teeth too."

Roger had a big heart—and an even bigger desire for people to come to Christ. He loved giving away little surprises—mostly candy—to bless whomever he'd meet during the day. When Rita posed her request, Roger admitted he had to give it some thought. She might not want the candy, but maybe the other women liked it.

So one Sunday Roger went to the church service the rescue mission held. He put small rolls of Life Savers under the seats of all the church attendees. Then he sat in the back row waiting for some action. He got some, all right. People crowded around him after church asking if he was the "life" saver. He was proud to say "Yes!" He told them he'd felt the prompting of the Holy Spirit to give each person a little gift.

Rita, however, wasn't so happy. Roger felt her impatience when she approached him after church. "I doubt the Lord would tell you to keep giving people candy that adds weight and cavities. I asked you to bring fruit."

Roger smiled, placed a hand on Rita's shoulder, and quipped in his inimitable style, "But I did, Rita. I took care of you and the other ladies. I gave out candy with fruity flavors."

Today's Thoughts

*Do not be quickly provoked in your spirit,
for anger resides in the lap of fools.*

ECCLESIASTES 7:9

I'm happy, dear Lord, that you keep me from blowing my top when I disagree with people. May I speak words of peace and understanding in every situation.

48

A Happy Surprise

Marion and her neighbor Ginger check up on each other and their husbands every day by email to be sure everyone's okay. Marion sends Ginger a message each evening, and Ginger responds first thing the following morning. If neither hears from the other, they check in person.

One evening Marion closed her email to Ginger with an encouraging line: "May your day bring a happy surprise!" Then she went to bed and slept soundly.

The following morning Ginger sent her usual email to Marion.

Marion decided to make a dozen blueberry muffins—something she rarely did. While they were baking, she felt a nudge from God. She remembered that Ginger's husband, Jim, was particularly fond of blueberry muffins. Marion phoned next door and asked if they'd like a few for breakfast.

The couple was thrilled. Minutes later Marion trotted over to their house with a basket of warm muffins right out of the oven. As she made her way back across the yard it suddenly hit her. "My gift of muffins was the happy surprise I wished for Ginger last night in my email message!" Marion chuckled, looked to the heavens, and sent God a mental high-five.

Today's Thoughts

*With long life I [the LORD] will satisfy him
and show him my salvation.*

PSALM 91:16

How blessed I am, dear Lord, that even if no one on earth looks out for me you always do. I praise your holy name!

49

Sweet Potatoes

Cynthia walked into the Save-A-Lot Grocery Mart and was pleased to see sweet potatoes on sale at a good price. She knew they'd keep well through the winter, so she bought a whole bag. She took them home and stored them in a cool bedroom, along with some apples and oranges she'd purchased.

She served the fruit in various recipes during the Christmas holidays, and planned to use the sweet potatoes for Christmas dinner. But because her daughter brought a sweet potato dish to that meal, Cynthia put her sweet potatoes on hold, knowing they'd be fine for another few weeks.

Following the holidays, Cynthia moved some of her furniture around, swapping certain pieces from one room to another. Months went by and Cynthia decided one night to bake a sweet potato as part of her supper. She looked for the bag of potatoes in the bedroom where she was sure she'd put them. They were nowhere in sight. Then she remembered she'd moved things around, so maybe they were hiding somewhere. She let out a sigh and set out on a mission to find the missing potatoes. Perhaps they were in another room now, but which one? The garage or even the storage unit were possibilities. Cynthia phoned her daughter to see if she'd seen them when she was visiting over the Christmas weekend.

Madeline said no, but she was amused at the situation and wished her mom luck in locating them. Her daughter assured Cynthia that by this time the "fragrance" of the potatoes should lead her to them.

Cynthia continued her search for another few days without success. "I said a prayer, asking the Lord to help me find the misplaced sweet potatoes," Cynthia admitted. Months passed and at Easter the following year, Cynthia's son and his wife were coming for dinner. Her daughter-in-law called ahead to ask if she could make sweet potatoes to go with the ham Cynthia planned to serve. Then she told her mother-in-law that a bag of sweet potatoes had mysteriously popped up at their house. She and her husband were sure they'd never bought them.

Cynthia burst out laughing. "Apparently my son grabbed the bag of sweet potatoes along with my Christmas gifts to his family when they left for home! And then they got misplaced at their house too. Mystery solved! Thank you, God."

Today's Thoughts
Put your hope in God.
Psalm 42:11

This story makes me smile, Lord. I've done so many silly things too, including misplacing a pair of earrings, a summer hat, and a bag of cherries I was sure I'd brought home from the grocery store. But when I put my hope in you, dear God, you get right to it and solve my problem. Thank you for taking such good care of me.

50

Trying to Be Helpful

Zach and Ellen plopped down on the two remaining seats near the boarding gate for their flight to New Zealand. They were bushed! They'd been up half the night packing and making sure they had all the documents and currency they needed. Boarding passes, passports, driver's licenses, itinerary, traveler's checks, and some cash. Then there were medications, vitamins, sleep aids, socks in case their feet got cold, extra jackets for cool evenings, and some playing cards and snacks for the long flight.

Finally, they'd fallen asleep at midnight and were startled when the alarm clock sounded at 4:30 AM—giving them a few moments to eat a bite, splash a bit of water on their faces, and pack up the remaining items before calling a taxi for the airport.

Finally they had time to take a breath and rest before the boarding call. "I could use a cup of strong coffee about now," Ellen muttered.

Zach turned up his hearing aid. His wife never drank coffee, so why would she start now? He decided he must have heard her incorrectly. He wanted to help, so he stood up and wandered down the aisle of vendors.

He stopped in a candy store and found what he was sure Ellen would love. After paying for it, he headed back to the gate. Before sitting down, he handed his purchase to her. "Here you go, love. Enjoy, but don't eat too many or they might upset your tummy this early in the morning."

Ellen frowned. "What are you talking about?" She took the box from her husband's hand, read the description, and burst out laughing. A Cup of Toffee! She opened the package and, sure enough, there was a coffee cup crammed with individual pieces of toffee candy. She looked at her husband and shook her head.

"I asked the clerk, and she said this was as strong as it comes. I hope it'll be all right."

Ellen plucked a candy from the cup, unwrapped it, and popped it into her mouth. "Perfect," she said. Then she offered one to her husband. *Life is certainly a new adventure after your mate starts wearing hearing aids,* she decided.

Today's Thoughts
A gentle answer turns away wrath.
Proverbs 15:1

Thank you, Lord, for reminding me to be gracious and patient when things turn out differently than I'd hoped, or planned, or asked for.

51

With and Without

Jackie and Kel, now in their sixties, decided to run a half marathon—21 kilometers (21k). It seemed like a good idea at the time, but when it came down to training, well that was another matter. It was much more fun to talk about than to do it, even though both had been following exercise regimes most of their adult lives. Still—competitive running had not been part of their routine.

At their ages, tight thighs, smooth calves, beautiful biceps, and slim waists were things of the past. Or were they? Maybe, just maybe, they could recapture some of their enviable physical traits—if they got serious about what they had to do to compete. The two friends headed for the gym.

Jackie pumped iron while Kel jogged on the treadmill. Then they challenged themselves to four times up and down the steep staircase. By the time they finished, they were ready for naps or pieces of pie or both! Instead, they took hot showers, dressed for the day, and walked toward the front door.

Kel looked at Jackie. "How about we celebrate our decision to run the 10k with a cup of soup at Dena's Deli?"

Jackie laughed and nodded, but added, "Without the bread and butter."

"And with a slice of pie for dessert," Jackie said.

"But without the ice cream," Kel said, agreeing to the plan.

"And with a cup of tea," Jackie added.

"But without a lump of sugar."

Jackie's face drooped. "Sounds dreadful!"

"I agree," said Kel. "Easy fix. Let's drop the withouts and you're on."

The pair locked arms and skipped out to the parking lot with a lot of enthusiasm but without discipline.

Today's Thoughts

No discipline seems pleasant at the time, but painful.
Later on, however, it produces a harvest of righteousness
and peace for those who have been trained by it.

HEBREWS 12:11

Lord, I see myself in this story. I have good intentions, but I don't always follow through. Help me keep my word to you, to others, and to myself.

52

Not So Bad After All

Patsy woke up with a hot, sore, swollen throat. She staggered into the bathroom and opened the medicine cabinet. *Where are those lozenges?* she questioned, knowing she'd bought a fresh package not long ago in case she caught a cold or the flu. They were her favorite flavor— orange—and had just the right amount of sweetening to make them bearable when her throat was as sore as it felt today.

She poured herself a glass of warm water and padded down the hall to the kitchen. She'd just have to make due gargling with saltwater. That was her dad's remedy every time she complained of a sore throat when she was a kid. Patsy shook her head at just the thought of salty water touching the blazing flesh in her throat. But if it worked for her father, she figured it would work for her too.

Patsy reached into the pantry and pulled out a bag filled with crystals. She poured a half teaspoonful into her glass and stirred. Then she took a deep breath, closed her eyes, and took in a mouthful to swish at the back of her throat. Even before she tasted it, she thought, *Ugh!* Then she had a surprising revelation! The concoction didn't taste as bad as she'd expected. It didn't burn at all. In fact, it felt cool on her delicate throat. She opened her eyes and decided to repeat the process. When she reached for the bag on the counter, she realized she'd taken out a container of sugar! No wonder it didn't burn. Patsy chuckled and decided this particular senior moment was actually a good one.

Today's Thoughts

Heal me, LORD, and I will be healed;
save me and I will be saved,
for you are the one I praise.

JEREMIAH 17:14

Lord, I do the silliest things sometimes. As I get older, I'm finding I'm less apt to get mad at myself because I know you will set me straight. I'm glad you're with me night and day and will warn me if I start to do something dangerous. Thank you for that.

Foodies

53

Under a Tack!

Eighty-two-year-old Maura and her daughter Penny walked into their favorite restaurant. Maura could hardly wait to order her regular meal—Mexican Chicken Salad. The waiter greeted them warmly and started them off with ice water, tortilla chips, and salsa. The women chatted and laughed as they exchanged news before the server came and took their salad orders. They hadn't been together for a couple of months, so there was much to talk about.

Penny filled in details about her high-school-aged children, and Maura brought her daughter up to speed about all that was going on at Hillside Senior Living.

The salads arrived and Maura dug in eagerly, munching away on the corn strips and lettuce. A moment later she gasped and put her fingers into her mouth.

Penny immediately reached across the table and touched her arm. "Mom, what is it? You're as white as snow."

Maura pulled out a bright yellow tack and held it up for her daughter to see.

Just then the waiter came by to check on them.

"How did this get into my salad?" Maura asked.

"Oh my goodness!" the waiter said between gasps. "That tack was in your salad? It must have fallen off the bulletin board in the back." With that he turned and raced back to the kitchen. A moment later the restaurant manager arrived at the table, gushing an apology.

"Madam, I am so sorry. Let me make it up to you." With that he handed Maura a gift card for a free meal the next time she visited the restaurant.

Not really hurt, Maura enjoyed the attention. Now she likes sharing her story, telling how she was "under a tack" that day at the restaurant. She recommends everyone order "a salad with tacks" because it comes with a free lunch.

Today's Thoughts

Do not withhold good from those to whom it is due,
when it is in your power to act.

PROVERBS 3:27

Lord, this incident was amusing—but also kind of scary. I'm grateful you kept Maura safe. Thank you for watching over me too.

54

Awful Waffles

Henry loved waffles for breakfast more than oatmeal, scrambled eggs, or Cheerios. His wife, Edna, tried to interest him in something different—just to mix things up a bit, but he'd always say, "No, thanks. Waffles it is." When she set the plate of fluffy cakes in front of him, he got right to it. First, he slathered each one with butter and then filled each little square with just the right drops of pure maple syrup. After that step he dusted each one with powdered sugar that he'd carefully sifted prior to sitting down at the table.

This ritual became very annoying to Edna. Just once in their 40 years of marriage she'd have enjoyed doing something different—like going out to breakfast or trying a daring new recipe. But Henry didn't budge. So one day Edna took matters into her own hands.

Henry came down to breakfast on a Monday morning and asked his usual question: "What's on the griddle? Those awesome waffles of yours?" Then he slapped his knee and laughed as though they'd never had this exchange before.

Edna murmured, "I'm not so sure about awesome. I'd say *awful.*" Then she relented and made the waffles her husband loved so much. She handed them to him already bathed in butter, maple syrup, and powdered sugar. Only something happened that particular morning that changed everything. By mistake, Edna had grabbed and used a bottle of soy sauce instead of pure maple syrup!

Henry took one bite and exclaimed, "All right, Edna. You win! These waffles are awful."

Edna looked at him quizzically. "What do you mean?" Then she realized the mistake she'd made with the syrup. She apologized. "Let's go out for breakfast—to the Waffle House," Henry said. Edna quickly grabbed her jacket before he changed his mind!

Today's Thoughts

The righteous eat to their hearts' content.

PROVERBS 13:25

Lord, thank you for providing abundance in every way—food, clothing, shelter, caring family and friends, and, most of all, your eternal love and compassion.

55

A Plateful of Love

Emily stepped up to the chef's table in the upscale dining room and admired the beautiful food spread. She could order eggs cooked in any form—with trimmings to boot. An omelet with tomatoes and cheese and olives and mushrooms and bacon sounded fabulous. She never prepared such intricate delicacies at home. Why not give in and have the works?

But then she thought better of the idea. She'd vowed before setting foot on the cruise ship that she would not overindulge. There was more to a cruise than food. Or was there? "You only live once," she chided herself softly.

Then she noticed a phrase on the menu board that was new to her: *Huevos Ahogados*. "All right," she decided. "I'll give it a go."

She ordered the dish and returned to her table with her order number. A waiter would bring her the food as soon as it was ready.

Minutes later a young man balancing a tray of breakfast treats stopped at her table. "One order of *Huevos Ahogados*," he said.

"Right here," Emily said, raising her hand slightly. "Thank you," she said as the waiter slid the hot plate in front of her. "I'm curious," she said, eyeing the eggs covered in a semi-thin salsa. "What do the words *Huevos Ahogados* mean?"

"Drowned eggs," the waiter replied.

Emily flinched. "Drowned? What a peculiar word for such an attractive dish."

"Drowned with love," he added.

"Mmmm, that's my kind of cooking!" And with that Emily picked up her fork and dug into her plateful of love.

Today's Thoughts
You will have plenty to eat, until you are full, and you will praise the name of the LORD your God.
JOEL 2:26

It's fun to try new dishes and to enjoy the plenty you provide, Lord. Thank you for always giving me what I need.

56

Iced Water

Daniel sat down at his assigned table in the dining room of Mission Hills Senior Living. He looked at his tablemates and smiled. What would they be up to today? Every meal seemed to bring up a new issue—whether a spill, or a mistake in food choice, or a misspoken word that caused hurt feelings in another. He vowed to keep a low profile himself. He didn't need any more to handle. Being old was enough!

Just then Jason, their waiter, came by and took beverage orders. The words "iced tea" echoed around the table. It seemed all four wanted the same drink. *Good. Off to a fine start!* Daniel thought.

Each person ordered his or her lunch—soups and sandwiches or salads—and then sat quietly waiting to be served their food. Within minutes, Bill, the man with the long, white beard, piped up. "Where's my iced tea?"

"It'll be here shortly," Daniel asserted, trying to head off a showdown between Bill and Jason, something his table companion was likely to take on if he didn't get his way when he wanted it. Minutes passed and lunch was served. Still no iced tea for anyone. Now Daniel was getting hot under the collar. He spoke to the waiter the next time he passed by the table, water pitcher in hand. "We each ordered a glass of iced tea."

"And we've been waiting quite a long time now," said Emily, the woman on Daniel's left.

"Sorry about that. I'll get right on it." The waiter disappeared, but soon returned with a bucket of ice cubes and a pitcher of water. He dropped a few cubes into each of the four glasses, plopped a tea bag on top of the ice in each glass, and then covered that with cold water. "Enjoy!" And with that he sailed away to the kitchen.

"Well, I'll be!" Bill said. "I'm going to report him the minute I finish my iced water!"

"I guess this memory thing is contagious," said Daniel. "Jason's been hanging around us old folks so long, he's becoming one of us—a member of the Senior Moments Club—even if he is only 21."

Daniel's friends all laughed and agreed.

Today's Thoughts

The LORD is the stronghold of my life.

PSALM 27:1

Lord, when situations and people annoy me, please help me say what I mean...but not say it meanly. Patience and compassion are always in order regardless of the circumstances.

57

Half Full?

Sheila had a ritual, and she liked to follow it without fail. When sitting at a dining table, whether at home or at a restaurant, she always ordered two glasses of liquid—to be served half full. *Never* up to the top. If a waiter made that mistake and served a full glass or showed a generous spirit by pouring just above the halfway mark, Sheila would ask him to start over and do exactly what she wanted. She simply didn't get why servers couldn't do it right the first time. (They probably wondered about her too.)

When asked one day why she preferred her orange juice, or milk, or soda to be served in half-glass portions, she said without missing a beat, "I look at life as a 'glass half full,' and I'm married to a man who has a 'glass half empty' point of view. This custom of mine is a reminder to me to always see life, no matter how old I get, as half full. That means there is more life to live, and it's my choice how I fill the rest of it."

"What about your husband? He'd look at your half-full glass and consider it half empty. Is that true for his life?"

"Yes! He sees his life as almost over, and he feels powerless to do anything to change it. Poor dear! But that's his problem, not mine."

With that comment, Sheila drank up and asked for a refill—a half refill, that is.

Today's Thoughts
A heart at peace gives life to the body.
PROVERBS 14:30

Lord, thank you for giving me life in *all* its fullness—no matter what the circumstances are and no matter who is in my life.

58

A Good Suggestion

Linda picked up a knife and tried to cut into the grilled chicken breast in front of her at Bob's Barbecue. "Must be a tough old bird like me," she commented with a chuckle. "It didn't even make a dent." She thought it was rude to pick up chicken and eat it, so she once again took the table knife to the chicken. It made a dent but didn't cut.

Her friend Harvey, sitting on the opposite side of the table, gawked. "Ask for another knife. That one must need a good sharpening. Or you can use mine, if you want." He handed his to her even as he licked barbecue sauce off his fingers on his other hand.

Linda waved it away. "No thanks. Your knife is gooey." She moved on to the buttermilk biscuit, eager to slit it open and smear it with butter and jam. The biscuit crumbled from the pressure of the knife—it didn't slice either. "Oh for pity's sake!" she murmured. "This is too much work. I should have ordered a bowl of clam chowder."

Harvey picked up Linda's knife to try it on his chicken. "Works perfectly for me," he noted. "Why don't you give it another try—this time with the cutting edge facing down?"

Linda's face flushed. Leave it to Harvey, a retired butcher, to figure out her mistake. She threw him a kiss and exclaimed, "My hero!"

Today's Thoughts

There is surely a future hope for you,
and your hope will not be cut off.

PROVERBS 23:18

Lord, how wonderful to have people close by who will help me even when I pull a silly stunt like trying to cut meat with the knife upside down. But it's even more wonderful that you are with me and in me. I'm never at a loss for your comfort and guidance.

59

A Little Service, Please

Frank and his wife, Katherine, moved to Brentwood Senior Homes for one specific reason: meals. Katherine would no longer have to cook, and Frank could have his choice of food at every sitting instead of having to eat his wife's cooking. He was ready for some variety after 50 years of marriage.

The first week they made friends with other residents and enjoyed sitting with them in the dining room. Frank especially liked being able to raise his hand and get immediate attention from the waitresses. A young woman would appear at his table and ask what she could do for him. What fun it was to say "iced tea," "apple pie," or "crackers and cheese," and *voila*! before he knew it his request was granted. He could get used to this excellent treatment.

One morning during a holiday weekend, traffic in the dining room was heavier than usual. The regulars were entertaining visiting family members, so the wait staff was particularly stressed. Half the waiters needed for such a crowd were serving double the usual number of people.

Frank raised his hand but no one rushed to his table. Annoyed, he raised two hands and still no response. Then he whistled.

Katherine tugged on his sleeve. "Knock it off, Frank. Can't you see how busy it is in here?"

"Yes, but I live here! And I'm paying big bucks for the privilege," he snapped. "Residents should have priority. What does it take to get a little service around here? All I want is a glass of ice water."

Finally, a young waitress with a nametag that read GINA stopped at Frank and Katherine's table. "Sir?"

"Ice water. Ice water," Frank said pointing at their glasses. "Our glasses are empty."

"Right away." Gina scampered off, and Frank settled down.

Gina returned with a bucket of ice cubes and plopped several into the empty glasses. Then she disappeared, never to return during the buffet meal.

Frank looked at his glass and sighed. "Guess this is the new way of conserving water. Give each guest a couple of ice cubes. When they melt they'll have the ice water they ordered."

Today's Thoughts
Be patient and stand firm...
Don't grumble against one another.
JAMES 5:8-9

Lord, every opportunity I get to extend grace to others who annoy me reminds me of your patience with me when I annoy you. May I look to you for the patience I need.

60

Peace at Any Price

Burt and Babs love Chinese food. In fact, whenever they go out to eat they inevitably choose an Oriental restaurant, and once or twice a month they order Chinese take-out. Noodles, fried rice, chow mein, and wonton soup are among their favorite dishes. Then comes the fun part at the end of the meal—breaking open the fortune cookies. Babs doesn't care much for the taste of the cookie, but the message inside is a fun surprise.

One Wednesday evening Burt walked in the front door from work hungry and ready to relax. "How about dinner at the Rickshaw and then a movie?" he suggested.

"Great idea. I have some things I want to talk to you about regarding the kids and grands. I think the family situation is getting out of hand."

Babs got Burt's attention with that statement. He'd hoped for a quiet, peaceful evening without any stress, but from what Babs just shared, this wasn't going to be the night for that.

They arrived at the Rickshaw, and Burt could feel the tension building. Babs seemed to sit on the edge of her seat through the entire meal. "What's eating at you?" he asked. "What have the kids done now? It's always something with that family."

"Today was the last straw. I called Melanie and invited her out for coffee. She agreed to meet with me for 40 minutes. Can you imagine? Not even one hour! How many people make dates with their mothers for an exact number of minutes? That's bizarre, if you ask me."

"Hey, Babs, aren't you being a little harsh? I mean she and Ben have pretty full lives with four kids, two dogs, two careers, and a big house to manage. I figure we're lucky to see them at all. Forty minutes is better than no minutes."

Babs blew out a breath. "I knew you'd take their side because Ben's your son and Melanie's not a blood relative."

"Don't start that again."

Babs lowered her head and pushed around the remaining rice on her plate. "But, Burt, not only did I get only 40 minutes of her precious time, but she played with her smart phone, cutting me off to take calls or respond to texts. What kind of visit is that? I've had it! You know how hard I've tried to be her friend. Well, I'm running out of patience and endurance." Babs dabbed her mouth with a napkin and reached for her fortune cookie. "Maybe there'll be some encouraging words in here." She split open the cookie and pulled out the slip of paper and read it aloud: "If you want to have peaceful communication with your loved ones, get a phoneless cord!"

Burt burst out laughing.

Babs cracked a smile. "I think I'll pass this on to Melanie."

Today's Thoughts

Wait for the LORD; be strong and take heart
and wait for the LORD.

PSALM 27:14

Dear God, you always have just the right words for me
no matter what I face. I thank you that I can trust you
in all things and in all ways.

61

An Unusual Tea

Crash! The china teapot hit the kitchen tile floor and sent Trudy into a tizzy. Everywhere she stepped shards crunched under her feet. How could she have been so clumsy—and with Janice dropping by any minute for tea and scones? What a mess!

Trudy carefully picked her way through the pieces of ceramic to avoid getting cut or spreading them further. She went to the closet and returned to the kitchen with a broom and dustpan. She swept up the debris and ran the vacuum to make sure not the slightest speck of broken teapot remained.

She glanced at the clock, let out a deep sigh, and then remedied the situation the best way she could think of. She filled her glass coffeepot with water and set it on the stove to boil. This would have to do until she could replace the teapot.

Within minutes the doorbell rang. Trudy opened the door to greet her neighbor. She invited Janice into the living room, where'd she'd set out two place settings on the coffee table, using her best china and delicate, lace-edged napkins. She decided not to say a word about the mishap in the kitchen. It was just too embarrassing. Plus she didn't want to hear any comments about clumsiness from her friend.

The women made small talk about their grown children, grandchildren, and hobbies. After a short while it was time to serve the tea and put out the scones. Trudy decided she'd pour the tea in the kitchen so Janice wouldn't see the container. She got up, excused herself, and went into the kitchen. "Milk and sugar?" she called to Janice over the divider between the kitchen and living room.

Janice nodded and said, "Yes, as usual. Two cubes of sugar and a dollop of milk."

Trudy returned with the cups and scones on a lovely blue tray, which she gently placed on the table in front of her guest.

Janice took one sip of tea as Trudy held her breath. Would her English neighbor detect that the tea had been brewed in a coffeepot?

Janice wrinkled her nose and squinted at her cup. "Mmmm. What an interesting flavor. I'm picking up just a hint of coffee in my tea." She paused. "I like it. I like it a lot. You must tell me where you bought such an unusual tea. I'd like to brew some myself."

Trudy stifled her gasp of relief. "It's my little secret concoction," she joked. "But I'm so glad you like it. How about a strawberry scone?"

Today's Thoughts

From six calamities he will rescue you;
in seven no harm will touch you.

JOB 5:19

Lord, what a Savior you are! You not only rescue me from my sins but also from myself and my often-clumsy behavior. Thank you.

62

Steak-Frites

"Mark, I know what I'm doing, all right?" Monica was determined to show her husband he could trust that she knew enough French to get them around France for a few days without starving. "For Pete's sake," she argued, "I took French for three years in high school. I ought to be able to order a decent meal. Relax!" She picked up the café menu.

Mark asked her to keep her voice down, and then said, "Well, keep it simple. I don't want you making a scene in this public place."

The two were quiet as they surveyed the options. Mark was at a loss as to what most of the words meant. Monica was firm in her opinion that she could order both of them delicious meals without any problems.

Mark whispered that he'd like a plain cheese omelet with a side of French fries. He slapped his knee and chuckled. "Can't come to France and not try French fries!"

The waiter appeared at their table. *"Madame, monsieur? Vous voudriez?"*

This was Monica's moment to shine. She pointed to the word *omelette* and then to her husband, making sure the waiter knew it was for Mark. Then she ordered *coq au vin* for herself. While the waiter went to put in their order, Monica explained to her husband what she'd ordered was a French braise of chicken cooked with wine, *lardons*, mushrooms, and garlic. She further explained that *lardons* are pieces of bacon used to baste the chicken.

"What about the fries?" asked Mark. "I didn't hear you say anything about them. I'd like the big kind—you know, steak fries. The kind I get at Julio's back home."

"I'm sorry," Monica said. "I forgot, but it's not a problem." She glanced at the menu again and noticed *steak-frites. They have them. Good!* thought Monica. She flagged the *garçon* and added to their order. *"Je voudrais des steak-frites."*

"Oui, Madame." The waiter hurried away.

"Pretty impressive," said Mark, patting Monica on the arm. "I'm sorry I doubted you."

Monica was feeling quite proud of herself...until the meal arrived.

Mark's omelet was fine, and the chicken dish looked wonderful. But why the big steak with the fries?

Monica did her best to ask the waiter why he'd brought the steak. By that time she was doubting her French.

"Steak-frites, Madame," He pointed to the meat and potatoes.

Then it dawned on Monica. *Steak-frites* must mean steak and fries! *"Merci, garçon."*

After the *garçon* left, Monica and Mark quietly laughed at the miscommunication and decided they'd need a take-home bag for sure with all the food in front of them. Monica doubted she'd be able to communicate that to the waiter, so she quietly wrapped the leftovers in her napkin and shoved the packet into her purse. Tomorrow they'd look for a McDonald's and hope it had a menu written in English. But before that, she'd call on God to dampen her pride and increase her humility.

Today's Thoughts

The LORD is near to all who call on him,
to all who call on him in truth.

PSALM 145:18

Oh, Lord, I sure can get myself into fixes when I venture out on my own without first asking you to guide my steps and my words.

63

Give Credit When Credit Is Due

"My treat," I said to my daughter, grandson, and sister as we paced back and forth in front of the food display at our favorite deli.

"I'll have the Blue Plate Special for kids." Miles was clear about what he wanted.

My daughter Erin browsed the selections and then chose polenta.

My sister chose a chicken wrap.

I selected three small salads.

We waited in line to check out. When it was our turn, the server piled trays with our food and slid them across the counter. My daughter picked up one, and I reached for the other after handing the cashier my credit card.

We maneuvered through the throng of people who were waiting for their orders or were in line to pay for their purchases. We found a table for four and settled in, each of us hungry and eager to eat.

My sister June slipped me a ten-dollar bill to apply to the total. I thanked her quietly and then dug into my salads.

Suddenly I felt a presence. Startled I looked up at a man who was towering over me.

He smiled as he put the credit card slip for me to sign on the table. I'd walked off without closing the sale!

How embarrassing, I thought. I signed the paper, handed it back, and returned my focus to my delicious salads and the wonderful conversation.

"Excuse me," the man interrupted. "Here's a little something you might need later today." With that he laid my credit card on the table.

Whew! Another moment of embarrassment. I was so grateful he'd been so conscientious and polite, when I hadn't been paying enough attention.

Today's Thoughts
The LORD longs to be gracious to you; therefore
he will rise up to show you compassion.
ISAIAH 30:18

Oh, these senior moments, dear God. They really do catch up with me even when I think I'm paying attention. I'm so grateful you have my back.

64

Shrimp for Two

Lois stood in the kitchen wondering what to fix for dinner. She looked in the pantry, then the fridge, and finally the freezer. Pizza, hot dogs, hamburger, salad fixings, beans, and rice were all there, but none of them appealed to her. Lois realized what she really craved was shrimp. She turned to her mother sitting on the sofa in front of the television watching the evening news. "Mom, I'd like some shrimp for supper. Does that sound good to you too?"

"Yes, it does! Good idea," Ruby said with a smile.

"That settles it then. I'll be back shortly, Mom. Go ahead and lay a place for each of us on the coffee table, and we'll enjoy our meal while we watch TV."

Lois took a deep breath when she stepped outside. She'd been in the hospital the week before, so it felt good to inhale the fresh air. Within minutes she pulled into the car line winding around the fast-food restaurant till it was her turn to place an order. She called to the man taking orders. "Sir, I'm deaf. I do wear a cochlear implant but still it's difficult for me to hear over this type of speaker."

"No problem, ma'am. What would you like to order?"

Just then Lois' mind went blank. For the life of her she couldn't remember why she'd chosen this particular restaurant and what she'd planned to order. She remembered craving a certain food, but what was it?

The young man at the window was waiting patiently for Lois to spit out her order.

Lois smiled and squirmed a little in her seat. She smacked her forehead. "Oh my! I forgot," she sputtered. "I'll think of it in a second, okay?"

"Don't feel bad, ma'am. You'd be surprised at how many people do the same thing."

Lois felt her face flush. "Good to hear that. I..." Just then she remembered and blurted out her order before it disappeared again. "Two shrimp dinners!"

She quietly thanked God the correct words had come to her just in the nick of time. She'd been thinking she'd have to drive all the way home and rehash her conversation with her mother before she'd remember what she'd craved. *Whew!*

Today's Thoughts
Commit your way to the LORD.
PSALM 37:5

Dear God, some of these senior moments are just plain fun—and some are totally annoying. Please keep me safe from those that create havoc. I know you can do this because you are with me morning, noon, and night.

Flying High

65

A Lethal Weapon

Rachel and her daughter Carol enjoy shopping and having lunch together a few times a year. During one shopping excursion, they were walking down the aisle of hats and handbags in their favorite department store when Rachel noticed a selection of beautiful purses. She turned to look at them more closely when suddenly she did what she calls her "purse thing"—swinging her shoulders so quickly that her shoulder-strap purse crashes into whatever is close at hand. In this case it was a spiral hat rack, and it went down with a clang.

An older couple came to her rescue, setting the rack back up, picking up the hats, and replacing them on the hooks. "My dear," said the gentleman, "you need to be more careful or you'll be taking home more than your share of hats and handbags—enough to last you the rest of your life, from the looks of it."

"You're so right," said Rachel. "Thank you for looking out for me."

"Oh, we weren't looking out for you," said the gentleman as he chuckled. "We were looking out for ourselves. You give quite a 'purse punch.' You'd better watch that weapon or you'll get yourself in more trouble than you're already in."

Rachel lowered her eyes and then glanced at the man. "I'll do that. Thank you for the warning." With that she turned quickly to look for her daughter Carol, and her purse fell from her shoulder and sailed off a short distance.

The same man she'd met a moment before came to her rescue

again, this time with a wink and a nod. "Ma'am, may I recommend a solution? How about purchasing one of these nice, compact clutch bags? It may be costly now, but it might save you the expense of a lawsuit later on."

Today's Thoughts

In this world you will have trouble. But take heart!
I have overcome the world.

JOHN 16:33

Lord, sometimes the trouble I get myself into is my own fault for not paying close enough attention or letting myself be distracted by the slightest thing. Thank you for not holding any of that against me and for gently guiding me back to reality.

66

The Weather Wins

My husband, Charles, and I sat on the plane, eager to get off the ground and wing our way from California to Ohio for Christmas with our daughter and grandkids. We hadn't enjoyed a Christmas holiday with that family in more than a decade. The pilot taxied the airbus out to the runway and then suddenly stopped and moved the plane to the side, announcing that a storm was blowing in to Salt Lake City (our connecting point), and we would be temporarily delayed until further notice.

We sat…and sat…and sat. Then the plane taxied back to the terminal as the flight attendant announced that all passengers were to disembark, but we should hang around the boarding gate for updates. We did that…and did it some more until word came that the airport in Salt Lake City was closed to all incoming and outgoing flights.

We hoped to be rerouted—as did the other 200 and some passengers who crowded the desk trying to make new arrangements. For us there was nothing available until two days later. So we returned to the departure area, picked up our baggage, and headed home to wait it out.

I was so disappointed I could hardly stand it. We'd just said goodbye to our clean house, cleaned-out fridge, lights all set on timers, heating unit turned down, and neighbors alerted about our absence. Now we had to buy food, turn on the heat, and tell the neighbors we were home again for two days. I pouted for a while and then decided to give that up and trust God to work all things for the good of everyone concerned. And when I left him to do what I couldn't do, he did just that.

Two days later we boarded, flew, landed, and enjoyed two weeks of fun and holiday cheer. When it was time to depart, we were spared the new storm that was threatening the Midwest. We drove to the airport just ahead of the heavy blanket of snow and got off the ground in the nick of time.

We nearly missed our final connection in Minneapolis. Once again I tossed up a request for guidance, and God came through as we were rushing from one gate to another. Suddenly a "tram angel," a driver with no passengers in his vehicle, appeared in our path. I stepped out in front of him and called, "We're old, we're in a hurry, and we're gonna miss our flight. Can you whisk us over to Gate F8?"

"Hop on!" he said. We jumped onboard, and he tooted his horn while scooting between the people as we hung on for dear life! He dropped us off just as the agent announced, "All parties may now board."

We made it home safe and sound—and full of gratitude.

Today's Thoughts

Let us not become weary in doing good, for at the proper time we will reap a harvest if we do not give up.

GALATIANS 6:9

Lord, I feel like giving up sometimes, but then I remember how you always come through in the right time in the right way. Thank you.

67

A Real Shaker

Sandra moved to California from Ohio with some trepidation. Having grown up in the Midwest, floods were no surprise to her—but earthquakes were another matter. She hoped she'd never have to endure one.

Shortly after settling into her new home, she awakened one night to a loud, lumbering noise. Her bed was shaking beneath her. She heard tree branches snap outside, and the window in her bedroom creaked. She feared someone had broken in and was hiding under her bed ready to pounce on her.

"I reached for my cell on my nightstand. I keep it handy in case of emergency," she shared. She was certain this event qualified! She phoned the police station. When the police answered, Sandra explained what was happening.

The policewoman chuckled and said, "Ma'am, you're okay. We're having an earthquake."

Then Sandra got really scared. The very thing she worried about and dreaded had occurred. But then she realized she was fine, and no real harm had been done. The bed was in the same place in her room, the window was still intact, and when she looked outside only a few twigs had broken off the tree.

Sandra explained that she was an Ohio girl—and earthquakes were foreign to her.

The two had a good laugh together and then hung up. Sandra went back to a peaceful sleep.

Today's Thoughts

*On my bed I remember you; I think of you through
the watches of the night. Because you are my help,
[God,] I sing in the shadow of your wings.*

Psalm 63:6-7

Lord, whether an earthquake, or fire, or flood, or hurricane, or tornado, you are my salvation and my hope. How I praise you!

68

Check In

Carly and her husband, Hank, were finally able to get away for a few days alone—something they really needed after a long harvest season on their farm. As usual, Carly took charge of the travel details while her husband made sure they had enough money in the bank to pay the airfare, hotel bill, and meals, with a little extra for some fun and souvenirs.

"Hawaii, here we come!" Carly whispered under her breath. The departure date was upon them, and they had only a few details to wrap up before taking off for the airport. To keep things straight, Carly made up a folder with all the necessary information—hotel reservation, flight times, an expense sheet, and a list of emergency telephone numbers in case something unexpected occurred. She had everything under control and was proud to tell her husband he had nothing to worry about.

After the five-hour flight from San Francisco, they arrived on the Big Island ready to play and relax. They rented a car and drove to their hotel, leaving their car and luggage with the bell captain while they walked to the front desk to check in.

The attendant scanned her computer file as the couple waited patiently. "I'm sorry," she said. "We don't have a reservation for anyone under your name. Are you sure you have the correct hotel?"

Carly's cheeks burned. "Of course, we have the right hotel. I have a printed confirmation right here in my purse." She rummaged through her shoulder bag and pulled out the pink folder with the hotel information. The date read July 8, not July 3! Carly's face fell. She had confused the numbers when making the reservations. Now what? They were thousands of miles from home. She started to cry.

"Please, ma'am. I'm sure we can fix this." The woman disappeared into the back room and came out a few minutes later with a smile on her face. "If you're willing to accept an upgrade to the honeymoon suite, it's yours."

Carly looked at Hank, and he stared back. They could barely afford a standard room—certainly not the honeymoon suite.

"I'm sorry but that's way over our budget. Is that the only option?" Carly put on her best pleading expression.

"Did I neglect to tell you it would be at no extra charge? No one has booked it for this week."

Carly switched to her best smile, and her husband gave her a squeeze. One silly mistake had turned into a fabulous surprise gift. Carly lifted her eyes to heaven. *God, you are so good! This is one senior moment I can live with.*

Today's Thoughts

*Every good and perfect gift is from above,
coming down from the Father of the heavenly lights,
who does not change like shifting shadows.*

JAMES 1:17

Lord, how great and good and giving you are. Your storehouse is filled with surprises that you give without measure.

69

Zoned Out

Simon and Mandy found two seats in the waiting area near their departure gate. They hadn't flown in a while, so Mandy handled her uneasy feelings with nervous chatter. Simon couldn't handle any more stress. Packing, driving to the airport, checking in, and going through security were enough for him to give up travel for good. To the grocery store and back was about as far as he'd be willing to go from now on. Where Mandy got this idea that they should take a trip to Washington DC, he couldn't understand. What would be so special about it? They could see all the monuments and statues and the White House on television from the comfort of their own home. "All that stuff is on a DVD!" he exclaimed when she'd posed the idea.

"It's not the same as being there in person," Mandy countered. "This is our nation's capital. We have to visit at least once before we die. Imagine! All that history packed into one city. I can hardly wait."

Simon took a deep breath and sighed. He knew she was going to win this one, so he agreed reluctantly. Now, as they waited to board the plane, he had to admit it did seem intriguing. Well, he'd see—when he got there. Meanwhile, he'd grab a snooze and get into line as soon as their boarding zone was called.

Suddenly, Mandy was shaking his shoulder. "Simon, it's time! The gate attendant is calling Zone 3. That's us!"

Simon sat up and snorted. He rubbed the sleep from his eyes and took a gander at the line of people leading to the Jetway. "We've got time," he said. "Look at all those folks ahead of us. It'll take a while for them to walk on, put their luggage away, and find their seats. What's your rush?"

Mandy threw up her hands and let out a long breath. "Simon, you do beat all, do you know that? Next time I go alone."

Simon caught his wife's hand and kissed it. "Just kidding." He stood up, grabbed his carry-on bag, and followed Mandy to the end of the line.

Mandy relented with a smile. "Hang in there, honey. Once you settle into your seat you can zone out till we arrive in Washington."

Today's Thoughts

You will go on your way in safety,
and your foot will not stumble.
PROVERBS 3:23

Thank you, God, for the gift of travel and for all the delightful places in the world I have yet to see and enjoy. Help me relish the opportunities you offer.

70

Famous for a Day

Claire enjoyed making the rounds at the Community Author's Fair that warm September day. It was always a pleasure to meet children from kindergarten to sixth grade and share with them details about "a day in the life of a real children's book author." The boys and girls seemed excited to meet her as well, and they welcomed her with hugs and handshakes and adoring facial expressions. She was a heroine in the eyes of many, and it felt good, she had to admit.

Teachers had prepared the students for her visit by introducing them to Claire's books. She wrote about homeless children, horseshoeing, natural disasters, and more. The boys and girls had made posters and scrapbooks celebrating her stories and picture books. They were on display in the gym, and Claire was eager to walk around the room and see their creativity on display.

She'd been writing for some 30 years and was about to turn off the computer and retire. Claire had earned her living writing, achieved some measure of success, and enjoyed years of visits to schools and libraries around the country. What more could a woman ask for in this autumn season of life?

As she strolled the halls going from one classroom to another, Claire felt her eyes misting. It was going to be more difficult to quit than she'd anticipated. Many of these students and teachers she knew well after so many visits, and they knew her. At least she thought they did.

At the end of the day, Claire returned to the front office, signed out, and said goodbye to the secretary. As she walked out the door, a little redheaded boy ran up to her. "Mrs. Mrs. wait! You're famous, aren't you?"

Claire's chest swelled as she considered his question. "I guess in my own small world of writing books I am famous," she answered.

But just as quickly, her chest sank when the boy continued. "What's your name?" he asked.

Today's Thoughts

Humble yourselves, therefore, under God's mighty hand, that he may lift you up in due time.

1 PETER 5:6

Dear Lord, there's no one like a child to bring a person back to earth hard and fast. Maybe that's why you remind us to become as humble as little children if we wish to enter the kingdom of heaven.

Wordy Ones

71

Half-Wits

John poked Margaret as they sat in the last row at a homeowner's meeting. They dreaded the hour-long process that always ended in squabbles and complaints. "Who's that guy across from whatshisname?" John whispered. "I know him but I can't think of his name. And what if he comes up to me afterward? I can't just say 'hi there' without including his name. How embarrassing."

"Shush!" Margaret clasped her husband's hand and put a finger to her lips. "Not now. It's rude to talk during the meeting."

"But think how rude it'll be if I can't remember his name. And it will be your fault for not helping me think of it."

"All right, but keep your voice down and eyes straight ahead. I'll start with the 'A' names, and you take it from there. Let me know when I hit the right one. "Andrew. Alan. Ace. Anson. Aaron…"

Margaret kept going, but John kept shaking his head all the way to the letter "H."

"I'm done," she murmured. "This is ridiculous. Just admit you forgot his name. After all you're getting older—and so is he. He'll understand."

"No! Look, Margaret, this has always worked before. Put our two 'half' wits together, and we'll be a complete wit! I mean…well, you know what I mean. We need each other."

Margaret put her hands together and tightened her lips. She let out a long breath and turned to her husband. "Enough is enough!" she whispered loudly.

The woman in front of them turned around and frowned. "Cut it out, you two. Have a little respect. The president is speaking, and I'm hard of hearing."

The president of the association finished his remarks and adjourned the meeting. John grabbed Margaret by her sleeve and pulled her toward the door. "Let's get out of here!"

"We can't. Look, here comes whatshisname. You have to face the music."

"Hi, there," the man said. "So good to see the two of you. It's been a while. Have you been traveling?"

"No, we've been around. You know, here and there with kids and grandkids and stuff." John's palms were suddenly wet.

The man put a hand on John's shoulder. "I'm really embarrassed to say this, but your name escapes me. Please forgive an old man."

"No problem," said John. "Happens to me sometimes too, doesn't it, Margaret?"

Margaret rolled her eyes.

"John. My name's John," he said.

"Now that's one for the books. Here we have the same name, and I can't even keep that in my mind. I hope you're doing better for your age than I am for mine!"

Margaret raised an eyebrow but didn't say a word.

Today's Thoughts

Those who know your name trust in you, for you, Lord,
have never forsaken those who seek you.

Psalm 9:10

As long as I remember your name and call upon it, I'll be okay, Lord. And, of course, you never forget my name. Thank you!

72

Our Know-It-All Friend

"Want to watch a movie?" Martin asked his wife.

"Sure. What do you have in mind?" Pam replied.

"I don't know. Something we can get into."

"Like one about WWII, right?" Pam asked.

Martin noticed her frown. "What's wrong with that?"

"We won the war, dear! Move on."

"I suppose you want to watch a 'chick flick' where the guy and gal are all lovey-dovey."

"What's wrong with that?"

"They're all the same. Girl flirts and connives until she gets the guy, loses the guy when he gets scared, and then gets him. End of story."

"That sounds pretty sarcastic. I seem to remember the plot differently. It's boy meets girl. Boy loses girl because he doesn't treat her right. Girl leaves. Boy chases girl. Boy repents and promises to change. Girl believes him. Boy proposes. Boy and girl get married. That's how we got together, isn't it? It's an age-old plot. It's what people like. And it has a happy ending. Viewers like that too."

"How about a movie about WWII that includes a boy meets girl loses girl gets girl in the end? Then we'll both be satisfied."

"Okay if you can find one. Good luck. I'm going to knit or read a book. Let me know what you come up with."

"I wouldn't know where to start. What do you recommend?"

"Ask our knowledgeable friend—the computer!"

Today's Thoughts

*Husbands, love your wives, just as Christ loved
the church and gave himself up for her.*

Ephesians 5:25

We're different—for sure—men and women, that is.
I thank you, God, for showing us how to meet in the
middle—at least sometimes.

73

Remotely Speaking

Jenny gets things done—on time or even ahead of time, and the work is always in tip-top shape. If someone needs something accomplished, she's the man...er...woman! She admits to being a "Type A" personality and a multitasker. She can juggle many plates at once and keep them going without a crash. That is, until...

One night as Jenny hurried home from a meeting, she was concentrating on the long night of deskwork she'd planned. She felt especially rushed and stressed. "I noticed the mail had arrived, so I jumped out of my car, gathered my purse and books, and pointed my car's remote keyless entry (RKE) at the car door. With a click, the door locked."

She made a quick dash to the mailbox at the curb and pointed her RKE once again. Nothing happened. She tried again as her impatience grew. "This is no time to act up!" she groused at the object in her hand. "I have work to do!"

She pressed the gizmo once more but still no change. How could she get to her mail? She was expecting a check from a client and needed to put the money into her checking account the following morning. One more try. Click! Click! Nothing.

Suddenly Jenny realized what she was doing—using her car remote for her mailbox. How silly was that? She glanced around to see if any neighbors were watching.

Just then a jogger ran by. "That's not going to work!" he yelled.

Jenny's face grew hot. She lowered her eyes, grabbed the correct key, opened the box, and reached for her mail. She closed the box and scurried into the house. But that wasn't the end of it. Days later she tried the same thing at the main post office when she stopped to pick up her ministry's mail. She returned to the car and explained to her husband what she'd done.

He came up with a possible solution. "You need a remote clicker to turn on your brain!"

Today's Thoughts

In all your ways submit to him, and
he will make your paths straight.

PROVERBS 3:6

Whew! I have so many close calls and embarrassing senior moments. Thank you for loving me and making sure everything turns outs okay.

74

What a Relief

Lucy's neighbor Manuel was a WWII veteran. He loved to tell war stories to anyone who'd listen. Lucy had been his audience of one on more than one occasion over the years.

Manuel took it on himself to see that his grandson Jake studied the piano. The grandfather paid Lucy to teach the boy. Every Wednesday Manuel and Jake came by, week after week. The boy improved and seemed to enjoy playing. Manuel was proud as punch, as he often admitted, that his grandson was taking up where he'd left off when he was a kid. "Not enough money for me to take lessons," he lamented one day, "so I want to be sure Jake has the chance I never had."

Lucy had a soft spot for the old man. His stories were a bit tiresome since she'd heard them all, but he had such a big heart she couldn't help but love and admire him for what he was doing for Jake.

At the end of each lesson, Manuel would knock on Lucy's door, ready to pick up Jake. Routinely he thanked her for what she was doing and gave her a big hug. Pretty soon Jake was doing the same.

One day Lucy teared up as Manuel wrapped his strong arms around her. "You're about the only one who hugs me these days," she blurted out.

Manuel stepped back and a puzzled look crossed his face. "I don't know why," he said as he patted Lucy's shoulder. "You don't smell bad."

Today's Thoughts

*The LORD makes firm the steps
of the one who delights in him.*

PSALM 37:23

Lord, you are a great God—bringing a smile to my face just when I need it.

75

Love that Little Child

Paul looked at Lulu, his sweet wife of 42 years, lying in the bed they'd shared all these years. She was pretty sick. Her face was pale and her hands looked frail. He loved her with everything in him, and he didn't want her to die. But he also knew that her time on earth was in God's hands so he needed to trust in the divine plan and not his own desire.

Pulling out his Bible, Paul began reading from Matthew's Gospel, chapter 18: "Truly I tell you, unless you change and become like little children, you will never enter the kingdom of heaven. Therefore, whoever takes the lowly position of this child is the greatest in the kingdom of heaven. And whoever welcomes one such child in my name welcomes me."

Paul started thinking about how people often referred to life in the older years—specifically the seventies and eighties—as a second childhood. That can feel like a cruel comment when a person is at that stage. But then Paul smiled, squeezed Lulu's small hand, and kissed her on the forehead. She did look like a little child in the middle of a big bed, so innocent and trusting. She couldn't do anything for herself anymore. It was up to God and him to do for Lulu what she could no longer do for herself.

Paul's eyes were suddenly wet with tears. He sank down on his knees beside his wife and wept. Then words so soft and quiet he almost missed them crossed his mind. It was as though they came straight from heaven…and maybe they did. "I love that little child." Paul relaxed his shoulders. He knew things were going to be all right.

Today's Thoughts

There is no fear in love.
But perfect love drives out fear.

1 JOHN 4:18

Lord, teach me to love and not give in to fear. Where love is, there you are.

76

Patience Relations

Rodney appeared at Oakhurst Memorial Hospital eager to start the volunteer work he'd signed up for with the Patient Relations Department. The work was easy enough. Just make the rounds, chat for a moment with the patients, and ask if they needed anything—a book or magazine, a prayer, a visit, a glass of water, help with the television or radio, or anything else.

He enjoyed people, wanted to be helpful where needed, and was glad to be of use now that he was retired from his teaching job of 40-plus years at the local high school. Rodney had experienced excellent health most of his life, so he felt compelled to serve those who were less fortunate. It took so little to bring a bit of joy to people who were suffering from cancer, or recovering from surgery, or being rehabilitated after an accident.

"Most of our patients respond well to the little things—a warm smile, a kind word, a funny story," said the department head, Mona, to the group of volunteers during a training session. "Rely on your intuition. You'll know what to do and what to say when you're there in person. Good luck and report back to me at the end of your stretch. Oh, and please know that you are very much appreciated. Thank you for your service." She concluded by reminding the volunteers to contact her immediately if they ran into anything out of the ordinary, such as a rude or belligerent patient. Rodney filed that remark away. He doubted he'd run into anyone he couldn't handle with a little humor.

The first few visits were a breeze. An older man asked for a particular magazine and a young boy enjoyed trading knock-knock jokes with Rodney. So far so good. He walked down the hall to the next room on his list—#415—and peeked in. "Hello!" he called to the woman in the bed. "I'm Rodney, and I'm here for patient relations. May I come in? And if there is anything I can do to make…"

Before he could finish, the woman in the bed bellowed, "How dare you suggest that you're here for patient relations! I'll have you know I'm a married woman. I only have relations with my husband!"

Today's Thoughts

Do not forget to show hospitality to strangers,
for by so doing some people have
shown hospitality to angels without knowing it.

HEBREWS 13:2

Even when we have good intentions, sometimes people question our motives. Help me, Lord, to do what is right in every situation. When I'm misunderstood, help me speak the truth in love.

77

Sign of the Times?

"Look, Mike!" Carrie pointed out a wooden plaque to her husband as they browsed a gift shop. "Let's buy it and hang it by the front door. The grandkids will get a kick out of it."

Mike picked up the wooden piece: "Grandparents at Play." He pulled out a 10-dollar bill and plunked it down on the counter by the front door of the shop. "I agree, and it's a fair price."

The two left the shop and headed home. They were bushed after a day of shopping and eating out. They were ready to crash in front of the television, feet up, popcorn bowl in hand.

But first Carrie had a chore for Mike. "Please hang up the plaque," she said. "It's a real conversation piece, and I don't want to forget about it."

Mike hustled to his tool drawer and pulled out a hammer and a couple of nails. In a matter of minutes the plaque was in place by the front door—just where Carrie wanted it.

That evening their daughter Jenny and her two kids, Shawn and Dede, stopped by unexpectedly. "We were in the neighborhood," Jenny said with a shrug. "I hope we're not interrupting anything. Just wanted to stop by and say hello."

Ten-year-old Shawn spoke up. "I like that plaque by the front door. It's new, right?"

"Yep. Bought it today," Mike said.

"What do you think?" asked Carrie.

Shawn frowned. "I'm not sure it fits you guys."

"What do you mean?" his mom asked.

"It says 'Grandparents at Play.' But Grandma and Grandpa are just watching TV."

"At our age, that's what we call 'play'!" Mike said.

Today's Thoughts
Their little ones dance about.
Job 21:11

Grandchildren certainly know how to bring us down to reality. I'm grateful for their honesty, hugs, and humor. Thank you, God, for my grands.

78

Hey, Sugar!

Roland liked two teaspoons of sugar in each cup of coffee, and he drank several cups a day—to his wife's dismay. Jane didn't like seeing him piling on the sweets at his age, but she couldn't do much about it.

While on vacation in England she hoped he'd switch to the preferred beverage there—black tea with a bit of milk and skip the sugar. But Roland wasn't easily persuaded. If there was a choice between coffee and tea, coffee won every time.

One morning after a restless night, Roland was eager to get to the dining room for his first cup of coffee. He turned to Jane. "I need a jolt to keep me awake during the tour today."

Jane rolled her eyes but zipped her lips. No use starting a quarrel first thing in the morning. She was intent on enjoying their vacation. When they arrived in the dining room, she focused on their table companions and made small talk about the agenda for the day. "I'm so excited about seeing Buckingham Palace!" she exclaimed. "I'm going to get a photo of Roland and me standing at the front gate. And I want a shot of those cute guards with their red trousers and tall, fluffy, black hats." She chuckled waiting for an acknowledgment from the couple sitting across from her.

At that moment, Roland looked around and blurted, "Where's the sugar? Looks like the waiter forgot to deliver it to our table."

"No, dear," said Jane. "It's over there." She pointed to the far corner of the long table. She stood up to reach for the bowl.

"Hey, sugar!" Roland said in a louder voice than usual, apparently happy to see the treat he needed to sweeten his coffee.

Just then the waitress rounded the corner next to where Roland was sitting. She stopped in her tracks and glared at him. "My name is Sara. I'll be happy to help you, sir, but please call me by my name. I'm not your sugar—or anyone else's for that matter."

Today's Thoughts
*I will instruct you and teach you
in the way you should go.*
Psalm 32:8

Whoa! People do get themselves into a muddle sometimes without knowing it. I'm so thankful that even when my words fly out of my mouth and land where I had no intention of sending them, you rescue me through your grace and wisdom.

79

It's a Wrap

Jeanette bought tickets to an open-air concert in Los Angeles. She rarely went out at night, but she couldn't resist this opportunity to hear one of her favorite bands. She was excited to be attending with her neighbor Rob. Both she and Rob had lost their spouses a month apart, so they found comfort in talking with each other and enjoying an outing together from time to time. Rob had treated Jeanette to a lovely dinner the week before, so she felt it was her turn to treat him. And since they both liked the same kind of music, this particular concert was well worth the money she'd spent.

Now for her choice of clothing. Jeanette browsed through her closet, eager to find just the right item—one that was nice but also warm since the cool night air would blow in just after sunset. A sweater? Maybe. A coat or jacket? Too heavy. She wanted something attractive, easy to put on and take off—a light wrap would do. But she didn't own anything like that.

Then she remembered her neighbor Sue, who lived on the other side of Rob's house, would likely have just what she needed. Sue was a fashion plate at age 72. "I don't think she'd mind loaning me a wrap for a few hours," Jeanette decided. She dashed off a text, knowing tech-savvy Sue kept her phone by her side night and day.

Within seconds Sue appeared at Jeanette's door with a package in hand. "Got your text," she said with a smile. "Here you go. It'll be the perfect snack before you leave for the concert."

"Snack?" Jeanette was puzzled.

"You asked for a wrap, right?" Now Sue appeared perplexed.

"Well, yes. You know—the kind you put around your shoulders to ward off the chill."

Sue burst out laughing. "Oh my! I thought you meant a wrap—you know, the kind you eat. I keep a supply in my freezer for quick meals. But I can get you a light-wool wrap, sure. I have those too!"

Jeanette joined her laughter. "I'll take both," she said. "And thanks for being such a well-prepared neighbor."

Today's Thoughts
It is more blessed to give than to receive.
Acts 20:35

What a cute story, Lord. Sometimes even when I want to be helpful and neighborly I get my signals crossed. Thank you for helping me navigate miscommunications with grace and mercy.

80

Facebook Fuss

Eleanor bragged that she didn't own a cell phone, or a computer, or an iPad, or any other tech device—and she never would, so there! One afternoon her grandson Conner tried to talk her into getting a simple email machine so she could stay in touch with her grandchildren.

"Grams, it is so easy to use and it's fun. Much easier than writing letters, especially now that you have arthritis." He worked hard at persuading her, but she wouldn't have any part of it. She stuck her nose in the book she was reading and sank down in the easy chair in front of the fireplace.

"Okay, have it your way. But I'd sure love to tell my friends that my hip grandmother knows how to text and use email and connect with me on Facebook."

"What's all this fuss about Facebook anyway?" she asked. "Why would anyone have to sign up for a way to talk to people when the phone has worked quite well for nearly a century? And what a goofy name. *Faaaacebooooook*." She mocked the word by drawing out each syllable. Then she held up the book she was reading. "See? I already know how to 'face book.' I face my book every time I pick it up to read!"

"Okay, Grams, you win." Conner blew out a long breath and returned to his laptop. *No winning with some of these older folks. And they tell us how hardheaded we teens are!*

Today's Thoughts

The tongue of the wise adorns knowledge,
but the mouth of the fool gushes folly.

PROVERBS 15:2

Lord, may I never become so stubborn and unyielding
that I refuse to learn something new that would ben-
efit me and those I love.

81

What a Crab!

Curt and Mame were invited to join some friends for Crab Fest at Fisherman's Wharf in San Francisco. Curt was especially excited about the event because he loved seafood. His wife? Not so much. She preferred food that grew on land. Still, she agreed to go. The event celebrated crab season by bringing together chefs from some of the best Fisherman's Wharf restaurants. They'd share bites of their favorite crab dishes and serve local beverages. Recipe ideas and a free commemorative cup would top off the evening nicely.

The couples strolled the wharf and browsed the gift shops before indulging in the delicious spread on the huge table under a canopy overlooking the ocean. Curt socialized with old friends and made some new ones. They talked shop and enjoyed bantering about golf, fishing, and the latest sports updates. Meanwhile, Mame found an open bench and seated herself there with a plate of salad. She'd never really liked seafood, so she was reluctant to try it again. But maybe she should, she decided, after watching people return to the table again and again and hearing remarks about how yummy the food was.

Mame got up and made her way to an empty spot in front of the array of crabmeat dishes and placed a few sample items on her plate. She returned to the bench and took a bite of two special recipes. Hmmm. Some of the concoctions, as she referred to the various blends, were actually very tasty. She went back for second and third helpings of her favorites.

Eventually Curt caught up with her. "I thought I'd lost you," he said with a scowl. "Where did you disappear to?"

"I didn't disappear," she said. "I was right here all along, hanging out with a bunch of crabs. And they are very nice—and tasty too," she said and winked.

Today's Thoughts

Everything that lives and moves about
will be food for you.
Just as I gave you the green plants,
I now give you everything.

GENESIS 9:3

Thank you, God, for providing what I need to keep physically fit. But even more important, you gave me the Bread of Life—Jesus Christ.

82

Questionable Company

Lloyd joined his new wife, Emma Jean, on her annual autumn visit to her son and his family in Alabama. It was his first time in the Deep South, and everything about it—from the food to the way people talked—fascinated him. He ate grits, collard and mustard greens, hushpuppies, pecan pie, finger-lickin' fried chicken, country ham, fried green tomatoes, and biscuits and gravy.

When the family ate out, Lloyd, a city man, let his wife order for him. He just couldn't make heads or tails out of the way folks spoke. They cut short some words and dragged out others. Trying to understand through their accent was driving him nuts.

After the visit was over, he finally felt the freedom to tell Emma Jean his thoughts about the trip.

"What did you think of my family?" she asked.

"Nice folks," he said.

"And the food?"

"Surprisingly delicious."

"And Alabamans in general?"

"Hospitable and friendly," he remarked. "But there is one thing I couldn't get the hang of."

"What's that?"

"So many derelicts to contend with."

Emma Jean scrunched her face in irritation. "What on earth are you talking about? Why, you'll not find on the face of the earth a nicer bunch of folks than Alabamans! I'm hurt by such a blunt evaluation of the people I love."

Lloyd scratched his temple. "Hold on, will you? I'm not talking about your family. I could understand them pretty well after a day or so. But when we went to the diner and to the grocery store and gas station, well, everyone talked just a little different, and I was racing to keep up with them. Good thing you were with me."

Emma Jean stopped for a moment and then laughed out loud. "Oh, you mean *dialect*—the way people talk."

"Isn't that what I said?"

"Darling, a *derelict* is someone without a home or possessions who has abandoned his or her responsibilities. I think you meant *dialect*. That word refers to a particular way of speaking that is specific to a region, such as the East Coast or the Deep South."

Now it was Lloyd's turn to laugh. "Oops! Sorry. I'd better get my wording straightened out or I may end up a derelict with a dialect in the Deep South."

Emma Jean nodded. "Sure thang," she drawled.

Today's Thoughts
[The LORD says,] "Before they call I will answer;
while they are still speaking I will hear."
ISAIAH 65:24

Lord, I have a lot to learn in every way. Thank you for giving me so many experiences and opportunities.

83

You've Got Mail

Harry sipped the strong brew in his favorite cup while he was wondering what was taking so long for his computer to warm up. It was old, for sure, but this was crazy. Suddenly the screen came to life, and Harry could finally look at the mountain of email he was sure to have after a long weekend out of town. One in particular caught his attention. It was a response to a request he'd made of the president of the book club to chair the team that would select books to present to the members for reading and discussing the next quarter.

He'd been reluctant to speak up before since the best that could be said about his relationship with Nick was that it was tolerable. Nick was always the one to have something to say about every book selected. Harry hoped Nick had finally recognized that he was as capable as anyone and would do an admirable job.

Harry read the message Nick left:

"It seems to me you're idle."

What? Henry flushed and his hands perspired. *Idle? He thinks I'm lazy? Well, I'll show him!* Then Harry read the closing sentence of Nick's email. "Get back to me right away, please." *That's strange to say after insulting me.* Harry called his wife to his side. He was boiling over by the time Patsy joined him. Quickly he summarized what he'd sent and what he'd just read. He admitted he was upset and asked her what he should do.

Patsy read the message and then broke out laughing.

"What's so funny?" Harry demanded. He wasn't feeling one bit amused.

"I think it's a typo *or* Nick doesn't know how to spell. I'm sure he means *ideal*, not idle."

"You think?" Harry's face lit up.

"Yes, I'm sure that's what he meant. Who could be more ideal than you, dear heart? So get to it. You're in charge."

Today's Thoughts

*If we confess our sins, [God] is faithful and just and will
forgive us our sins and purify us
from all unrighteousness.*

1 John 1:9

Lord, I feel bad when I jump to conclusions about other people and turn out to be wrong. Help me stay calm and patient even when people do insult me.

84

Con...conso...consol...

Sunny wished for all the world that she'd studied for her driver's license when she'd had the chance so many years ago. She also wished she'd taken computer lessons and had learned to use a smart phone. She felt hopelessly behind the times, especially now that her grandchildren were teenagers and had all the latest tech gadgets. How would she ever catch up with them, much less keep up? Was she the only senior who felt so left behind?

She sank into the old sofa that had held her aging body and eased her pain over the years since Herbie had died. What would her husband think of all this progress? He'd probably shake his head and then start talking about the "good old days" when people actually came to visit in person and sat on the porch and talked or played a game of cards while enjoying a bottle of Orange Crush.

Well, those days are over. Sunny tried to soothe herself out loud. "You'll just have to suck it up and carry on as best you can. Wasn't it President Teddy Roosevelt who said, 'Do what you can, with what you have, where you are'? Good advice!"

Just then her next-door-neighbor Greg stopped by. She invited him in.

"Sunny, I've been thinking you and I ought to grab a bite to eat and a movie tonight. What do you say? I could use a little company, and it seems you could use a little consolidation."

Sunny looked at Greg and let out a small smile.

Just then Greg caught his mistake of using the word *consolidation*.

"Oops! I meant to say you could use a little *consolation* since you live alone and all…since your husband passed. I hope I didn't offend you."

Sunny patted Greg on the shoulder. "No offense taken. And actually you're correct. I could use a little consolidation and some consolation too. I need all the strength and comfort you can offer. I'd love to join you for a bite to eat and a movie."

Today's Thoughts

If you devote your heart to [God]…
you will lift up your face;
you will stand firm and without fear.

JOB 11:13,15

Lord, some senior moments really are pretty funny. It seems more often than not we seniors are mixing up our words these days. Good thing we have your love to help us older folks forgive each other since we're all in this muddle together.

Slip-Ups

85

Far Enough

"Hon!" Beth called to her husband Rex. "Have you seen my glasses?"

"Doggone it, Beth, when are you going to be responsible for your own specs? I have a hard enough time remembering where I put mine. I think I'll start strapping yours to your head so they'll always be where they need to be—in front of your eyes."

"Very funny. Come on. I need your help. I'm running late, and I have to wash my hair." Beth was shouting over the pelting shower water as she massaged her scalp with shampoo.

"Seriously, babe!" he shouted from the bedroom, "This has gone far enough. You're on your own this time."

"Oh, yeah? Well how about you and your car keys? Who do you turn to every time you misplace them—which is just about every day? Me, that's who. Then I run all over the house like a maid checking this place and that, hoping I'll find them before you explode with frustration."

"Oh, pul-eeze! That's not the same thing at all. I do most of the driving, so it stands to reason that you share half the responsibility for the keys that operate the car. If I'm such a burden to you, then how about you becoming the keeper of the keys and doing more of the driving. Hmm? What do you think of that?"

Beth rinsed her hair, combing out the last of the tangles before stepping out of the shower. Her comb caught on something, and she tugged at it. Her glasses fell onto the shower floor. She burst out laughing. "I found my glasses!" she shouted. "No wonder I could see so well. I was wearing them in the shower."

Rex walked into the bathroom holding up his keys. "I'm sorry I got so upset. I found my keys. At least both of our lost items were where they should be—your glasses in front of your eyes and my keys in the bowl on my dresser.

Today's Thoughts
[God,] you guide me with your counsel.
Psalm 73:24

Thank you, dear God, for reminding me that humility is in order when I've had a senior moment.

86

Oh, Baby!

Rachel had given up driving. It was just too much at age 86. But it created a problem. When she ran out of things she needed, she had to ask her neighbor Debra to take her to the pharmacy or department store, as was the case one Friday morning. And Rachel didn't want to be a burden to anyone. On the other hand, she didn't want to be responsible for a bad accident...or, worse, a fatality.

"I don't understand why these teen grandchildren of mine—still babies, really—are so eager to drive," Rachel shared as her friend drove around a corner on the way to the store. "These youngsters are as much a menace to pedestrians as we old folks are—maybe more so. In fact, it's kind of nice to get old. I don't have to be responsible for so many things anymore. I can sit back and relax—read, nap if I want, and just take it easy."

Debra pulled into a parking space in front of the local drugstore. "I agree with you there. But personally I like driving. It gives me a feeling of independence. I guess I'm still a safe driver. No accidents in 50 years."

Rachel was secretly envious. Maybe she'd given up too quickly. If she hadn't turned in her license and sold her car, she could be driving to her sister's house, to the store, to church, and even to a movie once in a while. *Oh, well. Too late now.*

The two women slid out of the car and walked inside to pick up a few supplies. Rachel raised her hand. "I'll meet you at the checkout counter in a few minutes, okay?"

"Sounds good."

The two women went their own way, up one aisle and down another.

At aisle 12 they nearly careened as each reached for a box of Depends.

"Speaking of 'babies' driving!" chirped Debra. "I suppose those youngsters could accuse us of being unsafe drivers since we're clearly in our second babyhood. I depend on Depends, how about you?"

Both women had a good laugh and proceeded to the checkout counter.

Today's Thoughts

In Joppa there was a disciple named Tabitha...;
she was always doing good.

ACTS 9:36

Oh, God, how I thank you for caring for me whether I'm walking, driving, shopping, sitting, praying, eating, or sleeping. No matter what I'm doing, you are with me. What a comfort!

87

Savin' a Buck

Lottie and her cat, Pokey, had a love affair. Lottie, just like the pet food commercials say, would do anything for her pet. But she'd also do anything to save a buck. She traveled all over town, stopping at this pet store and that food mart, to be sure she was getting the most cat food for her well-earned dollar. She also clipped pet food coupons from the daily and Sunday newspapers for additional savings.

One Sunday she saw an ad for a 50-pound bag of cat chow. It made sense to Lottie to get in on this deal right away before the store ran out. She could get more meals per bag and, therefore, cut back on driving to the store so often. What a good idea! So she drove to the pet store in the next town to take advantage of the special. One of the clerks helped her load the heavy bag into the trunk of her car and off she went.

When she arrived home she realized something she hadn't thought of before. How would she get the hefty bag out of the car? In fact, how would she get it out of the car and up the three steps to her kitchen door? *Oh dear!* A real dilemma.

Lottie decided to compromise. She went to the kitchen and got Pokey's bowl. Carrying it out to the car, she opened the trunk, opened the cat food bags, ladled out a cupful, and poured it into Pokey's bowl. Then she sealed the bag shut and closed the trunk. She'd be hauling cat food into the house by the bowlful and around in her car until the contents shrank to an amount she could carry into the house. It might seem a bit odd, but at the same time she

figured she was being pretty clever. After all, she'd do almost anything to save a buck and this way of doing things fit that *cat*egory.

Today's Thoughts

*My flesh and my heart may fail, but God is the strength
of my heart and my portion forever.*

PSALM 73:26

God, thank you for supplying me with good ideas,
with plans, with solutions to problems that always
seem much bigger than I can handle by myself. Your
ways are not my ways—and what a good thing that is!

88

Out on a Limb

Matthew was feeling the aches and pains that frequently occur with old age and illness. The day came when he could no longer trim the trees or even change a light bulb.

His wife Lydia cracked a joke, hoping to cheer him up. "How many people does it take to trim a tree or change a light bulb?" she asked.

"More than I care to admit." Matthew tried to smile, but he was too upset to find any humor in the situation.

As the months wore on, the tree limbs were growing so long they touched the roof of the couple's carport. "I called a tree trimmer," said Lydia, "but he wanted too much money."

A day or so later, Lydia received a phone call from a young man and woman who wanted to get married right away. Although she was retired, Lydia occasionally performed pastoral work.

"Pastor, would you be able to perform the ceremony this afternoon?" the groom-to-be asked. "We're moving overseas for my job, and we want to be husband and wife before we take off."

Lydia didn't usually invite strangers into her house, but that day she felt a nudge to say yes. Lydia shared, "The couple arrived a few hours later with their rings, license, and other forms in order. Within minutes I joined them in marriage right there in our dining room."

Not long after, Lydia discovered the reason why the Holy Spirit had prompted her to say yes to the couple. John, the groom, was a tree trimmer by profession.

"When he heard our dilemma, he climbed onto the roof and trimmed the limbs. You can image our delight!" said Lydia. "Then he came back into the house and changed three light bulbs."

Now it was Lydia's husband who beamed. Two tasks taken care of in the same day, and two young people joined happily in marriage!

"I know God loves me," said Lydia, with tears in her eyes. "And I know he lives within my soul. But when he demonstrates his love in such a practical way, he is more real to me than at any other time. He is more than worthy of my praise."

Today's Thoughts
In their hearts humans plan their course,
*but the L*ORD *establishes their steps.*
PROVERBS 16:9

Lord, how amazing are your ways! You often guide my steps in ways I seldom expect.

89

A Tale of Two Earrings

"Have you seen my earring?" Phyllis asked her sister Irene in an email after a weekend visit. "I wore them at your house, but when I emptied my suitcase and all the little zipper pockets I had only one. The mate isn't in my purse either."

Irene promised to give the guest room and closet a good going-over, which she did after changing the sheets and towels and looking through the dresser drawers. She also checked the bathroom counter. "No luck," she wrote in an email. "So sorry for the loss."

Phyllis returned the message. "I'm sad. The earrings were a gift from my good friend Virginia. I'll have to explain it to her because she'll probably wonder what happened when I never wear them in front of her. I don't want her to think I'm unappreciative."

Irene agreed it was an unfortunate situation. After they hung up, Irene thought, *Maybe it fell out of Phyllis' ear when she turned her head, or nodded in a conversation, or leaned against the headrest in the car. That could be it! I'll check my car.* Irene hurried out to the garage and searched every inch of the front and back, including under and around the seats. She even used a flashlight to make sure she didn't miss anything. The earrings were black, so one would be easy to overlook. Once again, no luck.

Two months later, Irene and her husband were preparing for a weekend trip. Irene pulled out their luggage from the guest closet. She noticed a tiny object on the floor of the closet. It was so small she figured it was a dead bug snuggled against the back wall. She got a tissue and bent down to pick it up and throw it in the trash. But it wasn't an insect. It was her sister's missing black earring. Irene was overjoyed. She could hardly wait to call her sister and report the good news.

"Phyllis," she almost shouted into the phone, "you'll never guess what I found!" And she proceeded to tell her sister the details. But her sister didn't seem as enthusiastic as she should've been.

"Oh!" Phyllis finally said. "I just tossed out the matching earring this week since I had no hope of finding the missing one."

Irene let out a sigh, and then she got an idea. She'd buy Phyllis a new pair of black earrings for her birthday.

Today's Thoughts

Be strong and take heart,
all you who hope in the LORD.

PSALM 31:24

God, even when I'm disappointed I have hope because of who I am in your Son, Christ Jesus. He's the hope of us all. There is never a problem I can't solve when I walk with him and listen to his guidance.

90

Watch It!

"Ethel, what time is it? I can't find my watch anywhere!" Ray shouted from the den as he sat behind the daily paper in his favorite easy chair.

"What else is new?" his wife murmured. "If not the watch, it's something else." Ethel was getting increasingly annoyed with her husband's absentminded behavior and his reliance on her to remember for him. At age 81, she had enough to keep track of in her own life. But misplacing a watch? Well, she'd never do such a thing. It was important to her to know what time it was, and there was no better way to track time than wearing a wristwatch.

Ethel was in the bedroom changing the bedsheets. "It's time to start looking for your lost watch, that's what time it is!" she snapped.

Her husband's question sparked her curiosity about the time. She glanced at her wrist. *No watch. Oh, for the love of Pete. Don't tell me absentmindedness is contagious.* She rummaged through her jewelry box and the top drawer of her dresser, but her watch wasn't anywhere she could see. It didn't make sense. She always took it off at night and placed it on top of her jewelry box so it would be easy to spot each morning. Come to think of it, she hadn't worn it for a couple of days at least. Now what would she do? Would she have to confess to Ray that she too had misplaced a watch? *Never!*

Ethel made up an excuse to go for a walk, but she didn't need to bother because Ray had dropped the newspaper in his lap and fallen asleep. She'd be back before he woke up. An hour later Ethel tiptoed in the front door and took up where she left off—making up the bed in their master bedroom. As she shook out the top sheet something slipped to the floor. It was her lost wristwatch! Then it came back to her. She'd taken it off while doing the hand laundry so it wouldn't get wet. She must have swept it up from the counter along with the clean sheets.

Ethel slapped her forehead when she realized she'd just spent 50 dollars for a brand-new watch, which now she didn't need. She would have to return it. But first she said a quick prayer of repentance for judging her husband's behavior when she had the same problem. She also admitted her pride had gotten involved when she sneaked out to get a new watch so she wouldn't have to 'fess up. Ah, the sting of pride going before a fall.

Today's Thoughts
Pride goes before destruction,
a haughty spirit before a fall.
PROVERBS 16:18

It's so easy to judge others, Lord. It's time for me to put down the microscope and pick up the mirror!

91

Close Call

Katie had just about had it with her aging mother. She was losing one thing after another, and the costs of replacing the items were adding up. First a hairbrush, then a sweater, and now her hearing aids. The bean-sized gizmos cost nearly as much as a used car!

"Mom, I know it's getting more difficult to remember things," Katie said. "But I want you to try. When you put something down, just put it out on a table or on the bed so I can see it. I'll be glad to put it where it belongs so we can find it later."

Her mother nodded and lowered her head in shame.

Katie felt terrible. She wasn't so young herself, and her memory wasn't the best either. Why was she landing on her mom who needed her support not her criticism? Katie put her arms around her mother, hugged her, and asked for her forgiveness.

They sat down to dinner, and Katie did her best to make conversation. But it was no use. Her mother couldn't hear a thing without her hearing aids.

The following day Katie dropped everything she was doing when she heard a loud thud in the bathroom. She rushed through the door, and there was her mother on the floor on her backside. She'd tripped on a corner of a small bath mat. Fortunately she'd landed on the plush rug instead of on the hard tile. Katie's heart pounded as she helped her mother up and into a chair. She checked for bruises and anything broken, but everything looked okay.

"Mom, you're going to be okay," Katie reassured her, mouthing each word slowly so her mother could pick up what she was saying.

When she returned to her desk in the den, Katie decided she needed to consider enrolling her mother in adult daycare so she could be safe during work hours. Later, Katie walked into the bedroom and plopped down on the bed for a few minutes to pull herself together. Something poked her bottom. She jumped up and there was a pair of glasses, the delicate frames now bent at an odd angle and one of the lenses loose.

Mother! she shouted mentally. *Will this never end!*

Katie picked up the glasses and marched into the living room to give her mother another lecture about misplacing her possessions. She held up the frames to make her point and suddenly realized they were her own specs. She backed out of the room quietly, grateful she hadn't let her hasty remarks loose. "Like mother, like daughter," she admitted and then burst out laughing. "I guess we'll both be enrolling in adult daycare if I keep this up."

Today's Thoughts
*The fruit of the Spirit is love, joy, peace,
forbearance, kindness, goodness, faithfulness,
gentleness and self-control.*
GALATIANS 5:22-23

Lord, I feel overwhelmed when I face conflict and forgetfulness in myself or others. Thank you for your grace and mercy. Help me share those traits with others.

92

Double Trouble

Harriet was so nervous she was certain she'd fall apart. Her neighbor Jim had invited her on a date. She hadn't been out with a man for half-a-century—and even back then she certainly wasn't much for the nightlife. *What am I supposed to do? What should I order for dinner? I'm not sure what to talk about.* She worried herself with questions to the point that she was ready to call the whole thing off.

But then she got hold of herself and decided an evening out with a nice gentleman who was also a friend might be fun. There really wasn't anything to be concerned about. She, Jim, and his late wife had lived next door to one another for more than ten years. Now that Jim was a widow, he was probably lonely and simply wanted some companionship.

Harriet dressed, fixed her hair, and put on a little makeup. She looked in the mirror, turning this way and that. She decided she was still attractive. Her confidence rose. An hour later, she heard a knock at the door. She peeked through the peephole. Sure enough, it was Jim. She opened the door and there stood two men—Jim and a stranger. Her knees weakened and her heart pounded.

"What's up?" she asked, aware that her voice was shaking.

"This is my brother Dick," said Jim, clapping the man on his shoulder. "He's visiting for a few days, so I invited him along. You don't mind, do you?"

"No, I mean, sure. That is, all three of us on a date?"

Dick laughed. "What Jim is trying to say is that I have an old friend I'd like to see while I'm in town, so Jim offered to drop me off on the way to the restaurant with you."

Jim's face reddened. "Yes, he's just riding along with us, and then we'll pick him up at the end of our evening—if that's okay with you."

Harriet calmed down and smiled. "It's completely fine. I'll just grab a jacket and be right with you."

For a moment there Harriet thought she was in for double trouble! One man was enough—but two? No way!

Today's Thoughts
Better a little with righteousness…
PROVERBS 16:8

Lord, thank you for giving courage to the fearful, including me—especially when I'm presented with new experiences that you can use to help me grow.

93

Which Would You Choose?

"I'm ready for prison," Ed told his friend Sarah.

Sarah was shocked. "But you've never committed a crime in your whole life! Why would you want to spend your last years in jail?"

"I can't afford to be retired," Ed replied. "The cost of living is going up each year, and it's too much for me—even with my modest lifestyle. Just think about this, Sarah. It might work for you too:

- Free housing and three meals a day. That means no grocery shopping or cooking.

- No car so no gas, driver's license, or auto registration fees.

- No income tax and no jury duty. Yeah!

- Utility bills are on the prison, as well as lawn mowing, medical care, and entertainment.

- A clean uniform and underwear are provided.

"Doesn't that sound like a good deal, Sarah?"

"That's your idea of a happy retirement?" Sarah asked. "It's not mine, Ed!"

"Why not?"

"Because I already have all I need and want. My heavenly Father has provided well for me, and he always will. He's given me:

- *Rest:* 'Come to me, all you who are weary and burdened, and I will give you rest' (Matthew 11:28).

- *Love:* ' "Though the mountains be shaken and the hills be removed, yet my unfailing love for you will not be shaken nor my covenant of peace be removed," says the LORD, who has compassion on you' (Isaiah 54:10).

- *Security:* 'Do not be afraid, little flock, for your Father has been pleased to give you the kingdom' (Luke 12:32).

- *Parenting:* 'I will be a Father to you, and you will be my sons and daughters' (2 Corinthians 6:18).

- *Peace:* 'Peace I leave with you; my peace I give you' (John 14:27).

- *Assurance:* 'Even to your old age and gray hairs I am he, I am he who will sustain you' (Isaiah 46:4).

- *Salvation:* 'I give them eternal life, and they shall never perish; no one will snatch them out of my hand' (John 10:28).

"Now, doesn't that sound like everything you need?" Sarah asked. Ed looked at his friend. "You've got me there. I want the freedom you talked about. How do I get started?"

Sarah pulled out her Bible. She was more than happy to share God's Word anytime, anywhere.

Today's Thoughts
When calamity comes, the wicked are brought down, but even in death the righteous seek refuge in God.
PROVERBS 14:32

O, Lord, how faithful you are to house and feed me—in body and spirit. I want to praise your name forever.

94

Seeing Clearly

Buddy had a great idea for gifts for the relatives on his Christmas list. He'd take some great photos during the summer and fall and then frame them. He worried a bit, however, because his eyes were giving him fits of late, and he wanted to be sure he did a good job. Maybe it would help if he got a prescription for dark sunglasses so he wouldn't have trouble when he was shooting photos outdoors.

All went as he hoped. Soon Buddy was taking pictures of flower gardens, the trees in the nearby woods, and some of the exquisite architecture in his home city. After developing 100 or more of his beauties, he set out to place them in threesome frames so each person on his list would have two nature photos and one cityscape.

On Christmas afternoon he gathered with family and friends for dinner at his sister's house. After the meal he handed out his gifts and sat on the edge of his chair waiting to see the expressions on his family's faces when they opened them.

They were surprised, all right. But he was even more surprised! His sister Melanie opened hers first and held it up. "Very unique, Buddy. Thank you."

Oh my! Buddy saw something very strange. He'd placed the photos upside down in the frames. Of course, it could be fixed, but that's what can happen, he realized, when he wore dark glasses to do work that should be done in the light.

He was reminded of something the apostle Paul wrote in a letter to the believers in Corinth: "Now we see only a reflection as in

a mirror; then we shall see face to face. Now I know in part; then I
shall know fully, even as I am fully known" (1 Corinthians 13:12).

Today's Thoughts

Blessed are the pure in heart,
for they will see God.

MATTHEW 5:8

Lord, thank you that my silly, small mistakes can be
fixed easily and that my big ones can give way to major,
positive changes when I walk with you and keep you
as my focus.

95

The Deposit

Leslie opened her mail on Friday afternoon. She slit one of the envelopes and pulled out a check. "Yippee!" she shouted to her cat lounging in a sunny spot on the kitchen floor. She'd received a capital refund of $400 from the electric company. Surprised and excited, she decided to pay all her household bills before their deadlines. Leslie entered the amount into her checkbook and wrote several checks. She drove to the bank to deposit the check.

"I wanted to avoid the long line in front of the teller windows, so I opted to sign the check, put it into a deposit envelope, and pop it into the deposit-only box by the bank entrance. After I did that, I took off to mail the bill payments."

The following Monday an employee from Farmers Bank phoned Leslie. "We have your deposit here…"

Before the woman could say another word, Leslie blurted, "But, ma'am, I don't do business with your bank." She told the lady the name of her bank and was ready to hang up, when the woman stopped her.

"Wait! That's what I'm calling you about. I have your check for $400…"

Leslie interrupted her again. "I deposited that check into *my* bank."

Calmly, the woman continued. "You must have come to our bank by mistake. Remember, they're just across the street from each other. Would you like to come by and pick up your check? Or shall we return it by mail?"

"I'll come and pick it up," Leslie replied.

Later Leslie shared, "I had my doubts about what happened...until I returned the next day and drove into the Farmers Bank drive-thru. Sure enough, it looked very familiar. It had been my mistake. When I approached the bank manager, she was all smiles and said it could happen to anyone. I thanked her and left, feeling a bit chagrined at my senior moment but grateful to God for kind, honest people. The only thing I had to live through was my embarrassment."

Today's Thoughts

Praise be to the God and Father of our Lord Jesus Christ,
the Father of compassion and the God of all comfort,
who comforts us in all our troubles.

2 CORINTHIANS 1:3-4

Thank you, God, for seeing me through one embarrassing moment after another now that I'm a bit forgetful. If I asked you for guidance each morning maybe I would reduce my mistakes and multiply my feelings of peace. Remind me to do that, please.

96

Double Vision

"Peggy, I'm going to call Dr. Albert for an eye checkup," Reggie said as he sauntered into the den and plopped down on the sofa next to his wife. "The last couple of days have been terrible. I'm seeing double when I read. I guess it's time for a new prescription."

"That's pretty sudden." Peggy frowned. "You were just there two months ago. Now you've got me worried."

"Me too." Reggie lowered his head into his hands and let out a sigh. "Getting old is the pits. From one minute to the next I don't know what's going to happen. And I'm not just talking about the change in my vision. We don't need another medical expense right now."

After dinner Reggie sank into the sofa in front of the TV. "No more reading for me for a while." He set aside his newspaper and the novel he'd just purchased.

Peggy joined him with her knitting. She stroked his hand and kissed him on the cheek. "It'll be all right," she said. "We'll get through this together." She picked up her needles and the scarf she was working on, then suddenly put down the yarn. "What am I doing?" she blurted. "I can't knit without my specs. Where are they?"

"Don't ask me," Reggie said in a somber tone. "Mine are now totally useless so I can't help you search for yours."

Peggy walked out of the room and returned a moment later, carrying a pair of generic reading glasses she'd bought at the local pharmacy. "Whew! They were right where I left them—on the kitchen counter. I just forgot for a moment."

Reggie sat up. "Wait, those are mine." He reached for them but Peggy pulled back.

"No, I bought these a few weeks ago at West Side Pharmacy. You were with me, remember?"

"Oh my! I put them on this morning, and I couldn't read a thing so I got frustrated."

Peggy broke out laughing. "Well, that explains things. You were trying to read with these generics when you should have been wearing your prescription glasses." She poked him in the arm, and they both laughed.

Reggie blew out a breath. "What a relief. No appointment needed. Now all I need to do is find *my* glasses. What would I do without you, Peggy?"

Peggy patted his head. "I shudder to think of what would become of you!"

Today's Thoughts

Dear friend, I pray that you may enjoy good health
and that all may go well with you,
even as your soul is getting along well.

3 JOHN 1:2

Dear Lord, here I go again, jumping to conclusions about my health when you've got me covered. Thank you for taking away my fear and reminding me to trust you.

More Great Books by Karen O'Connor!

365 Senior Moments You'd Rather Forget

Gettin' Old Ain't for Wimps

Gettin' Old Ain't for Wimps! Gift Edition

God Bless My Senior Moments

The Golden Years Ain't for Wimps

Grandkids Say the Cutest Things

Grandma, You Rock!

Lord, How Did I Get This Old So Soon?

When God Answers Your Prayers

Grandkids Say the Cutest Things

Words to Warm Your Heart. Grandkids are amazing! Gathering a charming collection of their quotes and antics, gentle humorist and bestselling author Karen O'Connor hopes they'll brighten your day. These vignettes celebrate the candid comments and honest observations the young make about life, God, grandparents, and more.

You'll smile, chuckle, and even laugh out loud as you read these entertaining bits that are sure to remind you of the many cute things your grandkids have shared.

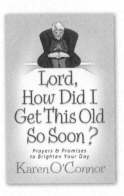

Lord, How Did I Get This Old So Soon?

Need a quick pick-me-up? Communion time with your heavenly Father? Author and humorist Karen O'Connor offers sincere, real-life prayers to encourage you to open your heart and talk with God.

> *Thank you, Lord, that it's never too late to dream a new dream, repair an injured relationship, make a new friend, draw closer to you...*

What I need right now is a big hug, Lord. Please hold me tight and remind me that you are always here for me...

My prayer is for strength today. I won't pray for a lifetime supply because I might go off on my own. I do best when I'm in touch with you daily...

Arranged by season to reflect the time of year or how you're feeling, these heartfelt prayers highlight the grace, mercy, and blessings God provides. You'll be encouraged by these thoughts that reflect where you are, reaffirm your hope during difficult times, and reveal how much Jesus loves you.